Revision Guide

to **AS Level Economics**

James Keefe and **Peter Cramp**

© Anforme Ltd 2008, revised 2012
ISBN 978-1-905504-21-3
Anforme Ltd, Stocksfield Hall, Stocksfield, Northumberland NE43 7TN.
Typeset by George Wishart & Associates, Whitley Bay.
Printed by Potts Print (UK) Ltd.

Contents

The first pages offer you advice on using this book. After this, you will find revision notes organised as shown below:

Unit 1:
(Micro)

AQA – Markets and Market Failure
Edexcel – Competitive Markets – How they Work and Why they Fail
OCR – Markets in Action

Chapter 1	Introduction to economics	1
Chapter 2	Production and economies of scale	7
Chapter 3	Demand and supply analysis	10
Chapter 4	Elasticity	16
Chapter 5	The price mechanism	22
Chapter 6	Market failure – monopoly	25
Chapter 7	Market failure – externalities, merit and demerit goods, public goods	28
Chapter 8	Market failure – imperfect information, immobility of resources, unstable commodity prices, lack of equity	33
Chapter 9	Government intervention – indirect taxes, subsidies, state provision	36
Chapter 10	Government intervention – price controls and buffer stocks	40
Chapter 11	Government intervention – regulation, extending property rights, tradable pollution permits	43
Chapter 12	Government failure	46
Chapter 13	Wages and the national minimum wage	48

Unit 2:
(Macro)

AQA – The National Economy
Edexcel – Managing the Economy
OCR – The National and International Economy

Chapter 14	Macroeconomic indicators	52
Chapter 15	Living standards and economic development	56
Chapter 16	The circular flow of income and aggregate demand	59
Chapter 17	Aggregate supply and macroeconomic equilibrium	63
Chapter 18	Consumption, saving and investment	68
Chapter 19	Economic growth	73
Chapter 20	Unemployment	76
Chapter 21	Inflation	81
Chapter 22	The current account of the balance of payments	84
Chapter 23	International trade and exchange rates	86
Chapter 24	Fiscal policy	89
Chapter 25	Monetary policy	93
Chapter 26	Supply side policies	96

Using this book

This book provides revision notes for both your AS Level Economics units.

For each unit, the relevant chapters follow a defined structure. It is important that you understand this structure.

The structure of AS Level microeconomics (**Unit 1**) is much the same for all exam boards:

Unit 1 – Structure	
Introductory concepts	Scarcity, factors of production, wants and needs, maximising behaviour, rationality, positive and normative economics and production possibilities.
Markets generally work well	Price Mechanism: Competitive markets allocate resources efficiently through the forces of supply and demand and setting the relative prices of goods.
Sometimes markets fail	Market failure occurs when markets fail to produce desirable outcomes, either because the allocation of resources is not efficient or because the outcome is unfair (there is a lack of equity).
This may justify government intervention	Governments may respond to market failure by intervening to improve the resource allocation or produce a more equitable outcome.
Government failure sometimes occurs	Government intervention is not always effective in achieving its aims. The costs of intervention may exceed the benefits, creating a loss of economic welfare. This is government failure.

The **Unit 1** chapters essentially follow this structure. Each chapter has a bar at the top highlighting where the particular chapter fits into the structure. For example, **Chapter 3** is about demand and supply analysis and is a building block in helping us to understand why markets generally work well and allocate resources efficiently. 'Markets generally work well' is therefore highlighted within the structure thus:

Chapter 3	Unit 1: Introductory concepts → **Markets generally work well** → Sometimes markets fail → This may justify government intervention → Government failure sometimes occurs
	Demand and supply analysis

If a particular chapter crosses over more than one bit of the structure, the relevant parts of the structure are all highlighted.

Contents

The first pages offer you advice on using this book. After this, you will find revision notes organised as shown below:

Unit 1:
(Micro)

AQA – Markets and Market Failure
Edexcel – Competitive Markets – How they Work and Why they Fail
OCR – Markets in Action

Chapter 1	Introduction to economics	1
Chapter 2	Production and economies of scale	7
Chapter 3	Demand and supply analysis	10
Chapter 4	Elasticity	16
Chapter 5	The price mechanism	22
Chapter 6	Market failure – monopoly	25
Chapter 7	Market failure – externalities, merit and demerit goods, public goods	28
Chapter 8	Market failure – imperfect information, immobility of resources, unstable commodity prices, lack of equity	33
Chapter 9	Government intervention – indirect taxes, subsidies, state provision	36
Chapter 10	Government intervention – price controls and buffer stocks	40
Chapter 11	Government intervention – regulation, extending property rights, tradable pollution permits	43
Chapter 12	Government failure	46
Chapter 13	Wages and the national minimum wage	48

Unit 2:
(Macro)

AQA – The National Economy
Edexcel – Managing the Economy
OCR – The National and International Economy

Chapter 14	Macroeconomic indicators	52
Chapter 15	Living standards and economic development	56
Chapter 16	The circular flow of income and aggregate demand	59
Chapter 17	Aggregate supply and macroeconomic equilibrium	63
Chapter 18	Consumption, saving and investment	68
Chapter 19	Economic growth	73
Chapter 20	Unemployment	76
Chapter 21	Inflation	81
Chapter 22	The current account of the balance of payments	84
Chapter 23	International trade and exchange rates	86
Chapter 24	Fiscal policy	89
Chapter 25	Monetary policy	93
Chapter 26	Supply side policies	96

Using this book

This book provides revision notes for both your AS Level Economics units.

For each unit, the relevant chapters follow a defined structure. It is important that you understand this structure.

The structure of AS Level microeconomics (**Unit 1**) is much the same for all exam boards:

Unit 1 – Structure	
Introductory concepts	Scarcity, factors of production, wants and needs, maximising behaviour, rationality, positive and normative economics and production possibilities.
Markets generally work well	Price Mechanism: Competitive markets allocate resources efficiently through the forces of supply and demand and setting the relative prices of goods.
Sometimes markets fail	Market failure occurs when markets fail to produce desirable outcomes, either because the allocation of resources is not efficient or because the outcome is unfair (there is a lack of equity).
This may justify government intervention	Governments may respond to market failure by intervening to improve the resource allocation or produce a more equitable outcome.
Government failure sometimes occurs	Government intervention is not always effective in achieving its aims. The costs of intervention may exceed the benefits, creating a loss of economic welfare. This is government failure.

The **Unit 1** chapters essentially follow this structure. Each chapter has a bar at the top highlighting where the particular chapter fits into the structure. For example, **Chapter 3** is about demand and supply analysis and is a building block in helping us to understand why markets generally work well and allocate resources efficiently. 'Markets generally work well' is therefore highlighted within the structure thus:

Chapter 3	Unit 1: Introductory concepts → **Markets generally work well** → Sometimes markets fail → This may justify government intervention → Government failure sometimes occurs
	Demand and supply analysis

If a particular chapter crosses over more than one bit of the structure, the relevant parts of the structure are all highlighted.

The notes for **Unit 2** (macroeconomics) also follow a defined structure:

Unit 2 – Structure	
Measuring the macroeconomy	The main four macroeconomic objectives (strong and sustainable growth, low unemployment, low and stable inflation and a satisfactory current account of the balance of payments) and how the corresponding indicators are measured.
How the macroeconomy works	The circular flow of income and aggregate supply/aggregate demand analysis.
Macroeconomic performance	Understanding the demand and supply side factors that influence performance with regard to the four main economic objectives. The difference between factors that affect the short run performance of the economy and the fundamental supply side determinants of long run performance.
Macroeconomic policy tools	Fiscal and monetary policies as ways of influencing aggregate demand and stabilising the economy. Supply side policy as a tool to influence trend growth and long term economic performance.

The chapter headings also work in the same way for **Unit 2** as they did in the first section of the book. For example, the chapter on living standards and economic development is about 'Measuring the macroeconomy' so this is highlighted accordingly:

Chapter 15

Unit 2: Measuring the macroeconomy → How the macroeconomy works → Macroeconomic performance → Macroeconomic policy tools

Living standards and economic development

Most of the material in the book is in common for all exam boards, but it may be helpful for you to have the specification (syllabus) for your exam board with you when you revise. We have tried to ensure that all concepts and theories on your specification are included in the book.

Occasionally there are concepts that are only specified by one of the exam boards. These areas are usually covered in their own chapters. So, for example, **Chapter 2** (Production and Economies of scale) is mainly for AQA students. **Chapter 13** (Wages and the national minimum wage) and **Chapter 15** (Living standards and economic development) are primarily targeted at Edexcel students. **Chapter 23** (International trade and exchange rates) is primarily for those following the OCR specification. However, these units may also be of interest to other students – you can never know too much economic theory!

We wish you good luck with your revision programme and your exams.

James Keefe and **Peter Cramp**

Chapter

1

Unit 1: **Introductory concepts** → Markets generally work well → Sometimes markets fail → This may justify government intervention → Government failure sometimes occurs

Introduction to Economics

Overview

One of the first questions students ask when they start a course in economics is why is there a need to study the subject? The simple answer is that there is a **basic economic problem** – there are only a limited number of resources available to satisfy our needs and wants. Thus economists must attempt to reconcile this problem of **scarce resources** and **infinite desires**.

Needs and wants

Man's physical needs are limited. They include food, water, clothing, warmth and shelter. Economists assume that man's wants are, in contrast, unlimited – for example, even a person who owns five luxury houses is likely to want more.

Factors of production (economic resources)

The **finite resources** used to produce output can be divided into four groups. Collectively, they are called the **factors of production**:

● **Land** – the natural resources on the planet. These include produce obtained from oceans and rivers, and as a result of a favourable climate. Minerals extracted from the planet, such as diamonds and aluminium, are also classified as land. Some natural resources are **renewables** (such as wind) others are **non-renewable resources** (such as fossil fuels).

● **Labour** – human resources used to produce goods and services. In the UK, there are around 28 million workers involved in the production process.

● **Capital** – items used by labour in the production process. Examples include factories, machines, roads and computers. All these capital items allow the production of goods and services in future time periods.

● **Enterprise** – the individual, or group of individuals, prepared to take a risk and combine the three other factors of production.

Each factor of production earns a reward, known as a factor payment. The factor payments are:

Factor	Payment
Land	Rent
Labour	Wages and salaries
Capital	Interest
Enterprise	Profit

The central purpose of economic activity is to combine factors of production (resources) to produce **output** for consumption. By satisfying needs and wants, the output produced generates **satisfaction or utility** and thereby increases **economic welfare**. Output can be subdivided into goods and services. Further subdivisions are possible. For example, goods can be either durable (such as furniture) or non-durable (such as food).

Economists take a fairly broad view of economic activity. Housework and DIY could be included, for example. They involve combining resources to produce valuable output, even if that output is not traded.

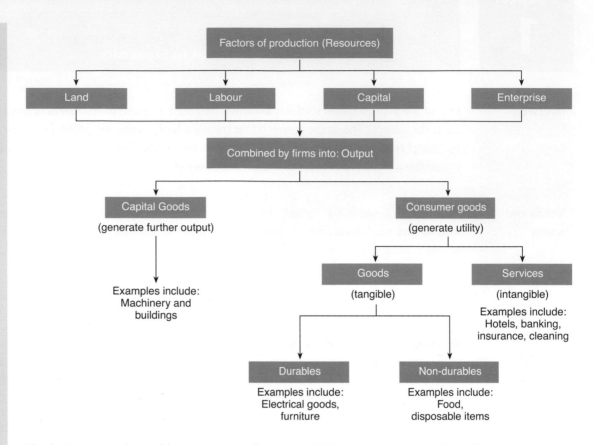

Scarcity and the economic problem

The basic **economic problem** is scarcity of resources. This occurs because society's finite resources are scarce relative to infinite needs and wants.

The basic economic problem means decisions must be made by society, or by individuals, about how to allocate resources. This involves answering three key questions:

1. What goods and services are to be produced?
2. How are they produced?
3. For whom are they produced?

Economic agents

The main agents (participants) in the economy are individuals such as **consumers** or **workers**, the **firms** who produce output and the **government**. All these agents have decisions to make regarding resource allocation.

Market economies

A market is any place in which a buyer and seller interact. This does not imply that the buyer and seller meet face to face (consider the market for items sold on e-Bay, for example). In a market economy, resources are allocated through the interaction of individuals and firms. The role of the government is limited to things like protecting people's rights to their property and issuing notes and coins.

In market theory, it is assumed that economic agents adopt **maximising behaviour**:

● Consumers try to maximise their satisfaction or utility from consumption, subject to the constraint of the income available to them.

● Workers try to maximise their income, subject to the constraint of wanting to enjoy leisure time.

● Firms try to maximise profits.

It is also assumed that economic agents are **rational**. If I choose to spend £20 on watching a football match rather than going out for a meal, it is because I gain more satisfaction or utility from the football match. The assumption of rationality rules out the possibility that I would have enjoyed the meal more than the football match and have simply made a mistake.

Here is how the three key questions posed by the problem of scarcity are answered in a market economy:

● The question of "**What goods and services are to be produced?**" is answered by the interaction of supply and demand in the price mechanism. There will be high demand for goods that generate high levels of satisfaction or utility. High demand forces the price of these goods up, giving an incentive to profit maximising producers to extend the supply of them.

● The question of "**How are they produced?**" is largely answered by firms. Firms are likely to seek the lowest cost methods of production in order to maximise profits.

● The distribution of income determines the answer to "**For whom are they produced?**". Those with more income will consume more goods than those with less income.

Mixed economies

Most economies in the world are mixed economies. This means that both markets and governments play a role in resource allocation. Governments intervene when markets fail to produce desirable outcomes (in other words, governments intervene to overcome market failures). The government sector of the economy is known as the **public sector**, while economic activity produced by other economic agents constitutes the **private sector**. The size of the public sector varies from one economy to another, but in the UK the government accounts for around 40% of economic activity.

Opportunity cost – the next best alternative foregone

The problem of scarce resources means that choices have to be made. As discussed in the previous section, this is true for individuals, firms and governments who all have to make decisions about how to allocate resources.

● An individual does not have an unlimited income and must therefore make economic choices on a daily basis. This could be whether to buy a new MP3 player or a DVD recorder. Workers must also decide if it is worth sacrificing leisure time so they can earn extra income to raise their standard of living.

● Firms may have to decide whether to use profits to invest in new machinery or to increase dividends to shareholders.

● Governments cannot spend infinite amounts of money on public services. They may be faced with difficult decisions, such as whether to increase spending on the National Health Service or on Education.

Such choices nearly always involve a cost. For example, the decision to purchase the MP3 player means that the DVD recorder will have to be given up. This is known as **opportunity cost** and is defined as **the next best alternative foregone**.

Economic goods and free goods

Economic goods are those that use scarce resources when they are produced, and therefore carry an opportunity cost. The only major resource on earth that is not scarce is the air that we breathe. This is called a **free good**.

Production possibility frontiers

A **production possibility frontier** (PPF) illustrates what an economy can produce using the resources of land, labour, capital and enterprise. It is useful in explaining the concept of **opportunity cost**. Consider the example of an economy that allocates all its resources to providing either manufactured goods or services. This is illustrated in Figure 1.1.

Figure 1.1

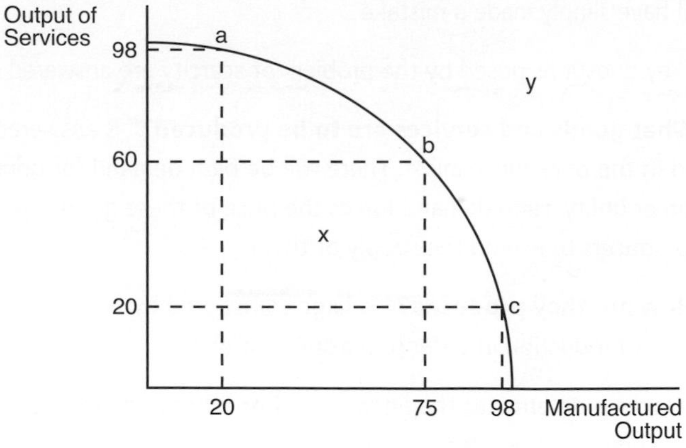

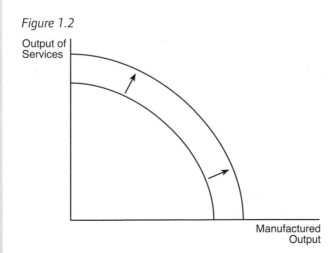

- Points a, b, and c all lie on the PPF and show maximum production when all economic resources are **fully employed** and used **efficiently**.

- Point x lies within the frontier and illustrates a situation where the factors of production are not fully employed and/or are being used **inefficiently**.

- Point y is not yet attainable given the current level of resources in the economy.

The production possibility frontier can be used to illustrate **opportunity cost**. The concave shape of the frontier indicates that the opportunity cost of manufactured goods in terms of services increases as more manufactured goods are produced.

If the economy were to **specialise** in producing manufactured goods, increasing output from 20 units to 75 units would lead to a relatively small fall in the production of services from 98 units to 60 units. The **opportunity cost** of the 55 unit increase in manufactured output is the 38 units of services that have been foregone.

Specialising even further, and increasing manufactured output from 75 units to 98 units, leads to a relatively large fall in the provision of services from 60 to 20 units. The **opportunity cost** of this small 23 unit rise in manufactured output is the 40 units of services that have been foregone.

This increasing opportunity cost can be explained by the fact that not all resources are equally suited to the provision of manufactured goods and services. The factors of production used in increasing manufactured output from 75 to 98 units are far better suited to the provision of services and this explains why the output of manufactured goods only increases by a relatively small amount.

Shifts in the production possibility frontier

Figure 1.2

Output of Services

Manufactured Output

The IT revolution has caused the PPFs of many economies to shift outwards.

In Figure 1.2, the PPF shifts outwards in parallel direction. This could have been caused by:

● An increase in the quantity of the factors of production – the shift may have originated from the discovery of new energy supplies, an increase in the active workforce or investment in new machinery.

● Improvements in efficiency or new technology – if there is an increase in the productivity of factors of production this will allow more output to be produced. The IT revolution of the last few years has caused the PPFs of many economies to shift outwards.

An improvement in new technology will not always cause a parallel shift in the PPF. For example, a new computerised production process will only impact on the manufacturing sector. The productive potential of the service sector will remain unchanged. This will lead to a shift in the PPF as shown in Figure 1.3.

Figure 1.3

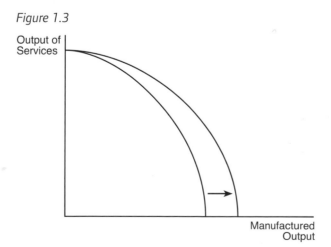

Specialisation (the division of labour)

Specialisation occurs at many different levels. Individuals may specialise in a particular occupation (Economics teaching, for example). Firms specialise (as Microsoft does in computer software). There are particular regional specialisations, such as pottery in Stoke-on-Trent, although such specialisations are increasingly under threat from international competition. Finally there are international specialisations.

China could be argued to specialise in manufacturing, for instance, while the UK has a strength in financial services.

Specialisation is a means of avoiding the need to be self-sufficient, thereby increasing output and living standards. We would all be materially worse off if we had to make our own clothes, build our own houses and grow or hunt our own food. It would be difficult to satisfy our basic needs, let alone to cater for the many desires that are satisfied in modern economies.

The specific **advantages of specialisation** are that it allows greater output for the following reasons:

● Workers can be assigned to tasks to which they are well suited.

● Workers 'learn by doing' and efficiency improves through experience.

● Production line methods save time changing tools.

● Production line methods may make it cost effective to provide specialist capital equipment for workers.

On the other hand, there are **disadvantages of specialisation**, such as:

● Boredom for workers engaged in repetitive tasks, which may in turn make them less productive.

● Regions or countries that specialise are dependent on other regions or countries for obtaining other products and services. This could cause problems in the event of trade disputes or wars between countries.

For specialisation to work well, it is vital that there is an **efficient means of exchanging products and services** with those who have other specialisations. The market economy serves this role well.

Normative and positive economics

There are two types of economic statements:

● **Positive Statements** – an objective statement. It is a statement of fact or a testable hypothesis (that is, a claim for which evidence to support or reject the claim can be gathered).

● **Normative Statements** – an opinion or view (in other words, a 'value judgement' about what ought to be, or should be, done).

For example, the UK's emissions of CO_2 are around 10% of that of the United States. This is a **positive statement** as it objectively describes a situation in the economy. The claim that an increase in duty on petrol would help to reduce emissions is also a **positive statement**. Support for the claim could be found in economic theory and empirical ('real world') evidence of what has happened in the past or in other countries when duty on petrol has been raised.

If an economist argued that the US should dramatically reduce its emissions; this is a **normative statement** as it expresses an opinion.

Chapter

2

Unit 1: **Introductory concepts** → Markets generally work well → Sometimes markets fail
→ This may justify government intervention → Government failure sometimes occurs

Production and economies of scale

This chapter is of special interest to those following the AQA specification. For those following the Edexcel and OCR specifications, a full understanding of the material in Chapter 1 on specialisation (the division of labour) should be sufficient.

The production process

The production process involves firms combining scarce resources to produce valuable output. The concept of efficiency focuses on the relationship between the resources used and the output produced. Efficiency in production implies maximising output from the resources used.

Productivity

Productivity measures output per input per time period. Thus labour productivity is measured as output per worker per hour worked, for example. This figure is calculated by dividing total output by the hours worked to produce that output.

Productive efficiency

Productive efficiency is achieved when waste is eliminated from the production process and the **average cost** of production is minimised (average cost is cost per unit of output, calculated as the total cost of production divided by output).

The private sector of the economy is generally thought to be more productively efficient than the public sector, because the profit motive gives private firms an incentive to reduce waste.

Any point on an economy's PPF is productively efficient, as shown by points a, b and c in Figure 2.1. Productive efficiency is also illustrated in Figure 2.2, which shows a textbook pattern of how average cost may vary with output. The shape of this curve is influenced by economies and diseconomies of scale.

Figure 2.1

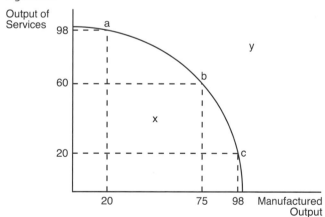

Economies of scale

Economies of scale are reductions in average cost resulting from the growth in size of the firm. Examples include:

● **Technical economies** – larger firms can employ and combine **specialist machinery** that should reduce the average costs of production. It may not be economically viable for smaller firms to purchase equipment that is highly productive because their output levels are too low to spread the cost of such machines. For example, a large supermarket could install bar code technology that will reduce the average cost of recording and ordering stock. It would not, however, be economically viable for a small corner shop to buy this technology.

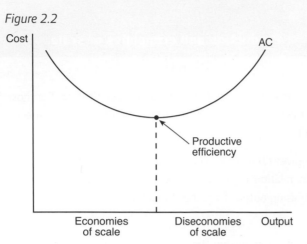

Figure 2.2

Within larger firms there is also greater scope for the **specialisation (division of labour)**. This is where the production process is split into many separate tasks allowing individual workers to become more proficient in their roles. The production line in many car plants is a good example of this concept. The increased productivity of the workforce will reduce average costs. See Chapter 1 for additional material on specialisation.

Another technical economy relates to the **law of increased dimensions**. This is linked to the cubic law where, for example, doubling the height and width of a tanker or building can lead to a more than proportionate increase in the cubic capacity. Examples of industries where this is important include:
- Food retailing
- Hotels
- Motor manufacturing
- Oil and Gas distribution
- Transatlantic Airlines
- Transportation
- Warehousing/Storage

- **Marketing economies** – as a firm grows in size it can spread its advertising budget over a larger output, but most importantly it can purchase its factor inputs in bulk at negotiated discounted prices. This is particularly the case when a firm has **monopsony (buying) power** in a market. The UK supermarket sector has exploited its position as the main buyer of produce from UK farmers and, as a result, has reduced the prices it pays for fresh foodstuffs.

- **Managerial economies** – larger manufacturers can employ specialists to manage and supervise production, thus cutting managerial costs per unit. For example, larger supermarkets can afford to employ specialist buyers who can reduce their buying costs significantly. Better management and the use of specialist administrative equipment, such as networked computers that improve communication, will raise labour productivity and reduce average costs.

- **Financial economies** – larger firms are normally perceived to be more credit worthy and therefore have greater access to credit facilities, with favourable rates of borrowing. Smaller firms often face much higher rates of interest on overdrafts and loans.

- **Risk-bearing economies** – larger firms may be able to purchase insurance more cheaply than smaller firms and may effectively be able to self-insure against the failure of any product line by diversifying to produce a number of different products.

Supermarket buying power has reduced the prices paid to UK farmers.

Diseconomies of scale

Diseconomies of scale occur when a firm grows beyond the scale of production that minimises average cost. The potential diseconomies of scale a firm may experience relate to:

- **Control** – monitoring how productive each worker is in a modern corporation is both imperfect and costly.

- **Co-ordination** – it is difficult to co-ordinate complicated production processes and they may break down. Achieving efficient flows of information in large businesses is expensive.

- **Co-operation** – workers in large firms may feel a sense of alienation. If they do not consider themselves to be an integral part of the business their productivity may fall.

Chapter 3

Unit 1: Introductory concepts → **Markets generally work well** → Sometimes markets fail
→ This may justify government intervention → Government failure sometimes occurs

Demand and supply analysis

Effective demand

Demand in economics must always be **effective**. Only when a consumer's desire to buy something is backed up by a **willingness** and an **ability** to pay for it do we speak of demand. For example, many people would be willing to buy a luxury sports car, but their demand would not be effective if they did not have the means to do so. They must have sufficient **purchasing power**.

Demand curves

Demand is defined as the **quantity** of a good or service that consumers are **willing and able to buy at a given price in a given time period**. For most goods there is an **inverse relationship** between the quantity demanded and the good's own price. This is illustrated in Figure 3.1.

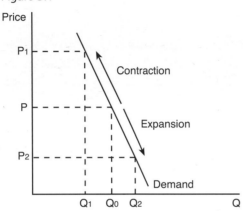

Figure 3.1

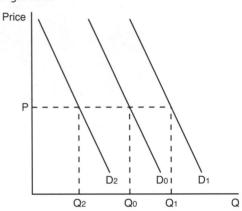

Figure 3.2

- A **change in the price** of the **good itself** causes a **movement** along the demand curve. For example in Figure 3.1, a **rise in price** from P to P_1 causes a **contraction** along the demand curve. Conversely, a fall in price from P to P_2 leads to an **expansion** in quantity demanded. These movements along the demand curve are usually caused by shifts in the supply curve, although they might also be caused by the imposition of specific prices by the government.

- A change in one of the **conditions of demand** will lead to a **shift** in the demand curve. This is illustrated in Figure 3.2. When the demand curve shifts to the right (D_0 to D_1) more is demanded at each and every price (Q_0 to Q_1). When demand shifts to the left (D_0 to D_2), there is a fall in demand for the product at each price level (Q_0 to Q_2).

Shifting demand curves – the conditions of demand

A change in any of the following conditions of demand will cause the demand curve to shift. However, remember: never shift the demand curve when the price of the good itself changes.

Conditions of demand include:

1. **Real income** measures the quantity of goods and services that a consumer can afford to buy. An **increase in real income** will cause the demand curve to shift to the **right** for the vast majority of goods that are classed as **normal**. However, some goods are **inferior** – this is where an increase in real income will cause demand to shift to the **left**. Examples of inferior goods may include rice, potatoes, tobacco and bus travel. An increase in income will cause the demand for bus travel to fall, as commuters switch to superior modes of transport such as private motor cars or rail services. The impact of a change of income on demand is analysed further in Chapter 4 when we look at **income elasticity of demand**.

2. Prices of other goods – Substitutes and Complements

Substitute goods or services are those in **competitive demand** that satisfy a similar need or want. Examples include different brands of soap powders, or types of crisps or soft drinks.

- A fall in the price of a substitute good will cause demand to shift to the left. If there is a fall in local rail fares (a substitute for bus travel), demand for train services will increase, but demand for bus travel will shift to the left.

Complementary goods or services are those goods and services that are often consumed together. They are said to be in **joint demand**. Examples include DVD players and DVDs, tennis racquets and tennis balls and package holidays and travel insurance.

- A fall in the price of a **complementary good** will cause the demand curve to shift to the right. If there is a fall in the price of new and second hand cars, the demand for these products will expand, and the demand for petrol (a complementary good) will shift to the right.

3. **Tastes and preferences** – tastes can be volatile, and often lead to a change in demand. A good example would be the large fall in demand for holidays to the USA following the 9/11 terrorist attacks. Fluctuations in consumer tastes can lead to big variations in demand at each price. This is particularly true for products that are fashionable for a very short period while there is a craze to purchase them. These goods are called **fads**.

   Standard demand theory assumes that consumer preferences are fixed – meaning that one person's preferences do not affect those of others. This is now being questioned. In many markets, the views of some consumers have an impact on the preferences of other consumers (either positively or negatively) – these feedback effects can mean that demand for certain goods and services becomes volatile and difficult to predict.

4. **Interest rates** – the level of interest rates affects the demand for many items, particularly 'big ticket' household durable goods (TVs, consumer electronics and dishwashers) and items typically purchased on **credit** (cars, home improvements and holidays).

   A rise in interest rates will reduce demand. Higher interest rates increase the incentive for consumers to postpone consumption and save their money instead. Higher rates will also increase the cost of loan repayments and discourage consumers from undertaking a purchase. Changes in interest rates also affect **consumer confidence** and therefore influence the willingness of consumers to commit themselves to major items of spending.

5. **Population changes** – a rise in population will shift the demand for most goods to the right. However, the age structure of the population is also important. The UK has an **ageing population** and, inevitably, the demand for products such as pensions, nursing homes and stair lifts will shift to the right.

6. **Advertising and Marketing** – a successful advertising or marketing campaign will shift demand to the right. This in itself makes the **price elasticity of demand** (see Chapter 4) for the product more inelastic.

Ceteris paribus

It is important to remember that the demand curve is drawn assuming **ceteris paribus**; that is, 'all other things being equal'. A change in any of the **conditions of demand** will result in a **shift** in the demand curve. Only a change in the **price of the good** itself will lead to a **movement** along the curve.

Why do demand curves slope downwards?

The main reason that demand curves slope downwards from left to right is because a fall in price makes the good cheaper relative to substitutes (this is called the substitution effect). The fall in price also increases the consumer's purchasing power and may encourage them to buy more of the good (this is called the income effect).

For a small number of goods, the demand curve may slope upwards.

Exceptions to the law of demand

Veblen goods – A fall in the price of a luxury product that is consumed for ostentatious reasons may result in a fall in demand. This is because as the price of the product falls it loses some of its snob appeal and kudos and consumers will switch to more expensive and exclusive products.

Giffen goods are very inferior products on which low income consumers spend a high proportion of their income. Basic foodstuffs in developing countries, such as rice, may be an example. When the price rises, consumers may not have enough income left to buy more expensive items of food that previously provided some variety in their diet. Instead, they buy more rice.

Supply curves

Supply is defined as the **willingness and ability** of producers to supply output onto a market at a **given price in a given period of time**.

There is usually a **positive relationship between supply and price**. As prices rise it becomes more profitable for existing firms to increase output and supply may be boosted further by the entry of new firms into the industry.

A change in the **own price of the good** (caused by a shift in the demand curve) results in a **movement along the supply curve**. A fall in price causes a **contraction**. A rise in price causes an **expansion**. This is illustrated in Figure 3.3. A change in one of the **conditions of supply** causes a shift in the supply curve. When the supply curve shifts to the right more goods are supplied at each and every price. This is shown in Figure 3.4.

Figure 3.3

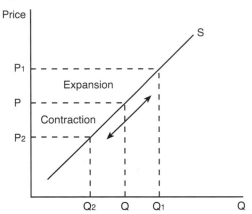

Figure 3.4

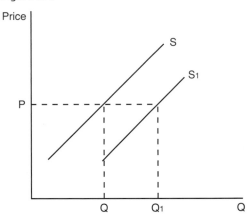

Conditions of supply

Just as with the demand curve, remember that a change in the price of the good itself does not shift the supply curve. However, the supply curve does shift when any of the following **conditions of supply** change:

1. **Prices of factors of production** – raw materials, components and wage levels. A fall in the price of paper would shift the supply curve for a newspaper producer to the right as more output can be supplied at each price. In contrast, for a haulage company, higher fuel costs would cause supply to shift to the left because fuel is an essential raw material.

2. **Productivity of factors** – an improvement in labour productivity means that each worker will be able to produce a higher level of output. This will reduce **unit labour costs** and shift the supply curve to the right. The efficiency gains may be partly passed onto the consumers in the form of lower prices.

3. **Indirect taxes or subsidies** – the introduction of VAT or additional excise duties on a good will shift the supply curve to the left. This is because taxes add to the costs faced by a producer. The supply curve of the airline industry has shifted to the left following the introduction of air passenger duty.

A **subsidy** encourages a producer to increase production. The grant or payment from the government will lower a firm's costs of production and shift the supply curve to the right. The supply curve of many agricultural commodities has been shifted to the left following a reduction in subsidies from the European Union.

4. **Producer decisions** – the aims of a business can affect its supply decision. For example, if a firm switched from **revenue maximisation** to **profit maximisation** this would cause the supply curve to shift to the left.

5. **Technological advances** such as the developments in robotics and information technology reduce the costs of production and shift the supply curve to the right.

6. **Prices of substitutes** – a rise in the price of a substitute will cause supply to shift to the left. Suppose the price of parsnips rose, this would encourage farmers to increase the production of this particular root vegetable and reduce the supply of others such as carrots and turnips.

7. **Entry of new firms into an industry** – the entrance of new firms into an industry shifts the supply curve to the right and puts downward pressure on the market price.

Market equilibrium

Market equilibrium occurs when the **market clears**, with supply equal to demand. This is shown in Figure 3.5(a) with the equilibrium price at P and the quantity traded at Q. The significance of the equilibrium price is that consumers are able to buy exactly the amount they wish to purchase at that price, while suppliers are able to sell the amount that they wish to sell. Consequently, no participant in the market has an incentive to change their behaviour: market equilibrium is a **state of rest**, with no forces acting to bring about a change in price. Market equilibrium will only be disturbed if one of the conditions of supply or demand changes leading to a shift in the relevant curve.

When there is a situation of excess supply or demand, the market is said to be in disequilibrium. Market **forces** then act to push the market back towards equilibrium.

Market forces

Figure 3.5(a)   *Figure 3.5(b)*   *Figure 3.5(c)*

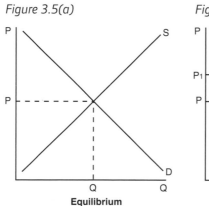
Equilibrium

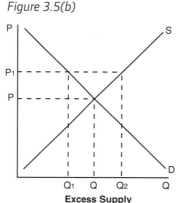
Excess Supply

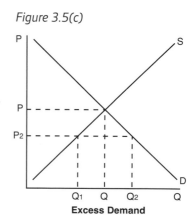
Excess Demand

Excess supply: In Figure 3.5(b), when prices are at P_1 there is **excess supply** (quantity supplied Q_2 is greater than quantity demanded Q_1) and firms will be forced to reduce prices in order to shed stocks. There will be an expansion along the demand curve and a contraction in supply until a new equilibrium is established at a lower market price P.

Excess demand: In Figure 3.5(c), when the price is at P_2 there is **excess demand** (quantity demanded Q_2 is greater than quantity supplied Q_1) and prices will be forced upwards as there is a **shortage** of the product. This causes an expansion along the supply curve and a contraction in demand until equilibrium is, once again, restored at price P.

**The effect
of a shift in
demand**

Ceteris paribus, **a shift in the demand curve to the right**, will raise prices **and** expand the quantity supplied.

Figure 3.6

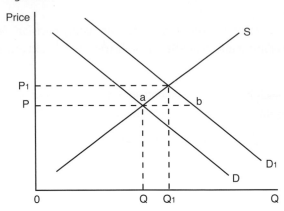

In Figure 3.6 it is assumed that the market for a normal good is in equilibrium at price P and quantity Q. Suppose there is now an increase in **consumers' real income** that causes the demand curve to shift to the **right** from D to D_1. At the **original price** P there is a **shortage** (a–b). This shortage will cause prices to be bid upwards and this will result in an **expansion or extension** along the supply curve until a new equilibrium is established at a **higher price** (P_1) and a **higher level of output** (Q_1). The more **inelastic the supply curve**, **the larger** the increase in price and the **smaller** the rise in output.

When **demand shifts to the right** the firm experiences a **rise in total revenue** (price x quantity). The shaded area in Figure 3.7 shows the increase in total revenue. At price P, the original level of total revenue is equal to $0PaQ$. Following the outward shift in demand, the new level of total revenue is $0P_1bQ_1$.

Although there is a rise in total revenue it cannot be immediately assumed that a firm's profit will rise. This is because there is also a **rise in the firm's total costs** as output has increased from Q to Q_1. In this instance the **effect on profit is therefore ambiguous**, since both revenue and costs have increased. It is impossible to tell accurately whether profits will rise or fall.

Figure 3.7

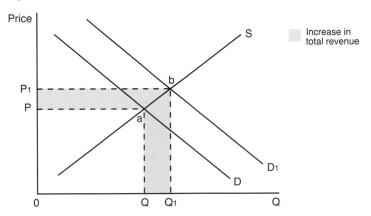

**The effect
of a shift in
supply**

Ceteris paribus, **a shift in the supply curve to the right**, will reduce prices **and** expand the quantity demanded.

In Figure 3.8, the market is in equilibrium at price P and quantity Q. Suppose there is now a technological advance which causes the **supply curve** to shift to the **right** from S to S_1. At the **original price** P there will be a **surplus** (a–b). Suppliers will lower their prices to reduce stocks and this will result in an **expansion** along the demand curve until a new equilibrium is established at a **lower price** (P_1) and a **higher level of**

output (Q_1). The more inelastic the demand curve the **larger** the fall in price and **smaller** the increase in output.

Figure 3.8

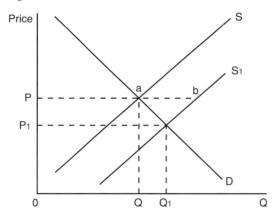

When **supply shifts to the right** the impact on total revenue depends on the price elasticity of demand (see Chapter 4). In Figure 3.9, demand is inelastic. At the original price P, total revenue was equal to the area $OPaQ$. Following the outward shift in supply, the new area of total revenue is equal to OP_1bQ_1. The fall in price from P to P_1 results in a fall in total revenue **because the area of loss exceeds the area of gain**.

The effect on profit in this case is clear-cut, as there is also a **rise in the firm's total costs** because output has increased from Q to Q_1. As the firm's revenue has decreased while its costs have increased, its **profit will fall**.

Figure 3.9

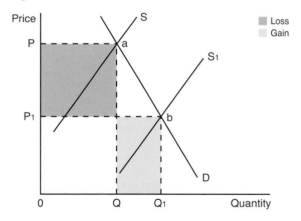

Chapter

4

Unit 1: Introductory concepts → **Markets generally work well** → Sometimes markets fail → This may justify government intervention → Government failure sometimes occurs

Elasticity

Price elasticity of demand (PED)

Price elasticity of demand measures the responsiveness of **quantity demanded** to a change in the good's **own price**. The formula for the calculation of PED is:

$$\text{Price elasticity of demand (PED)} = \frac{\text{\% change in the quantity demanded of good X}}{\text{\% change in the price of good X}}$$

Calculating PED

Consider the following demand schedule for buses in a city centre.

Price (average fare)	Quantity of passengers per week
100p	1,000
60p	1,300
30p	2,275

Suppose the current average fare is 100p, what is the PED if fares are cut to 60p?

The **percentage change in quantity demanded** is equal to:

● the change in demand 300 (1,300 - 1,000) divided by the original level of demand 1000. To obtain a percentage this must be multiplied by 100. The full calculation is (300 ÷ 1,000) x 100 = 30%.

The **percentage change in price** is equal to:

● the fall in price 40p (100p - 60p) divided by the original price 100p. To obtain a percentage this must be multiplied by 100. The full calculation is (-40 ÷ 100) x 100 = -40%.

These two figures can then be inserted in to the formula with 30% ÷ -40% = **-0.75**.

Let us now consider the PED when the average fare is cut from 60p to 30p.

The **percentage change in quantity demanded** is equal to:

● the change in demand 975 (2,275 - 1,300) divided by the original level of demand 1,300. To obtain a percentage this must be multiplied by 100. The full calculation is (975 ÷ 1,300) x 100 = 75%.

The **percentage change in price** is equal to:

● the fall in price 30p (60p - 30p) divided by the original price 60p. To obtain a percentage this must be multiplied by 100. The full calculation is (-30 ÷ 60) x 100 = -50%.

These two figures can then be inserted into the formula with 75% ÷ 50% = **1.5**.

There are some important points worth remembering when calculating PED:

● PED is a **real number**, not a percentage or fraction.

● The PED will **vary along a demand curve** and will depend on the **direction of the price change**. For example if the average bus fare were to rise from 60p to 100p, the PED would be 0.34. The percentage change in quantity demanded is 23% while the percentage change in price is 67%. When the price fell from 100p to 60p the elasticity was 0.75.

● The PED for all **normal goods** will be **negative** because a rise in price will cause a fall in quantity demanded and vice versa. When, however, we analyse the significance of the PED the **sign is often ignored**.

	Elasticity value	Description	Meaning
What do the elasticity figures tell us?	Zero	Totally inelastic	Demand is completely unresponsive to price changes
	Between zero and one	Inelastic	Demand responds less than proportionately to price changes
	One	Unitary elasticity	Demand responds proportionately to a change in price
	Between one and infinity	Elastic	Demand responds more than proportionately to a price change
	Infinity	Perfectly elastic	Demand is completely sensitive to the price. Any price increase causes demand to fall to zero

Diagrams for different PED values

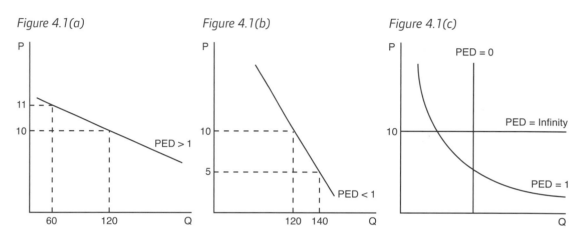

Figure 4.1(a) Figure 4.1(b) Figure 4.1(c)

- In Figure 4.1(a), the price rise from 10p to 11p results in a 50% fall in quantity demanded, which is greater than the 10% rise in price. The PED = 5. As this is greater than 1, the good is **elastic**.

- In Figure 4.1(b), the fall in price from 10p to 5p results in a 17% rise in quantity demanded, which is less than the 50% fall in price. The PED = 0.34. As this is less than 1, the good is **inelastic**.

Factors that influence PED

1. **Number of close substitutes within the market** – The more close substitutes available in a market, the more elastic demand will be in response to a change in price. A large rise in the price of one brand of washing powder will result in many consumers switching to one of the other brands. As a result, demand will be **elastic**. A large rise in the price of petrol will only lead to a very small fall in demand as there are no close substitutes. As a result, demand will be **inelastic**.

2. **Luxuries and necessities** – **Necessities** tend to have a more **inelastic** demand curve, whereas **luxury goods** and services tend to be more **elastic**. If prices rise, most consumers will only marginally reduce their consumption of necessities, such as bread, but they are more likely to cut back on their purchases of luxuries that they do not actually need. For example, the demand for opera tickets is more elastic than the demand for urban rail travel. The demand for holiday air travel is more elastic than the demand for business air travel.

3. **Percentage of income spent on a good** – It may be the case that the smaller the proportion of income spent on a good or service, the more inelastic demand will be. A 10% rise in the price of a good costing a few pence, such as matches, is more likely to be absorbed than a 10% rise in the price in the price of a good costing thousands of pounds. As a result, demand for more expensive items, which take up a large proportion of income, is likely to be more sensitive to price changes.

4. **Habit forming goods** – Goods such as cigarettes and drugs tend to be inelastic in demand. Preferences are such that habitual consumers of these products become de-sensitised to any price changes.

5. **Time period under consideration** – Demand tends to be **more elastic in the long run** rather than in the short run. This is because it takes time for consumers to adjust their spending habits following a change in price.

PED and pricing decisions

It is important for producers to know the PED of their output when making pricing decisions. Pricing decisions have a key impact on a firm's total revenue and profit.

● **Total revenue** = selling price x quantity sold.

● **Profit** = total revenue – total cost.

Price elasticity has a key impact on both variables.

● When a good is **price elastic** a **fall in price** will cause a **rise in total spending** on the good.

● When demand is **price inelastic** a **rise in price** will cause a **rise in total spending** on the good.

Figure 4.2

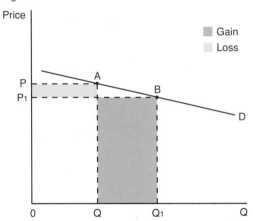

In Figure 4.2, demand is **price elastic**. At the original price P, total revenue was equal to the area OPAQ. Following the price fall to P_1, the new area of total revenue is equal to OP_1BQ_1. The fall in price from P to P_1 results in a rise in total revenue because **the area of gain exceeds the area of loss**.

Although there is a rise in total revenue it cannot be immediately assumed that a firm's profit will rise. This is because there is also a **rise in the firm's total costs** as output has increased from Q to Q_1. In this instance the **effect on profit is therefore ambiguous** as both revenue and costs have increased. It is impossible to tell accurately whether profits will rise or fall.

Figure 4.3

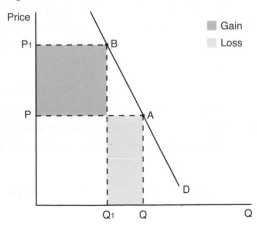

In Figure 4.3, demand is inelastic. At the original price P, total revenue was equal to the area OPAQ. Following the price rise to P_1, the new area of total revenue is equal to OP_1BQ_1. The rise in price from P to P_1 results in a rise in total revenue **because the area of gain exceeds the area of loss**.

The effect on profit in this case is more clear-cut because there is also a **fall in the firm's total costs** as output has decreased from Q to Q_1. As the firm's revenue has increased while its costs have fallen, its **profit will rise**.

Other uses of PED

If a firm knows the price elasticity of demand of its output it can use this information to calculate how much demand will vary following a change in price. Suppose the PED for baked beans is (-)0.4, it is possible to calculate exactly how much demand will fall following a rise in price.

The percentage change in demand = percentage change in price x PED.

If prices rose by 10%, then quantity demanded will fall by 4% (10% x -0.4) = -4%.

This information can be used by firms for **business planning**:

● to estimate changes in **production levels**.

● to identify whether **employment** in the firm will need to change.

● to analyse how changes in demand will affect **stocks**.

Income elasticity of demand (YED)

Income elasticity of demand measures the responsiveness of demand in percentage terms to a change in the **real incomes** of consumers.

$$\text{Income elasticity of demand (YED)} = \frac{\text{\% change in the quantity demanded of good X}}{\text{\% change in the real income of consumers}}$$

Normal and inferior goods

Normal goods are defined as those with a positive YED. Mobile phones, steak, air travel and foreign holidays are examples.

If the YED > 1, the good is considered to be a **luxury** and the proportion of income, or **budget share**, spent on the good rises with income. If the YED < 1, the good is considered to be a **necessity** and the **budget share falls** with income.

Inferior goods are defined as those with a **negative YED**. Examples may include bus journeys and own-label foods. When income rises, consumers may opt for superior alternatives in the form of private transport and branded food respectively.

Using income elasticity of demand

The value of an income elasticity is important to a firm as it determines the size of a **shift in demand**. Suppose a computer firm has two products, a desktop with an income elasticity of +0.5 and a laptop with an income elasticity of +3.5. If real national incomes are forecast to grow by 3% next year the firm can calculate the rise in demand for its products. Demand for desktops will rise by 1.5% (3% x +0.5 = 1.5%) and demand for laptops will increase by 10.5% (3% x +3.5 = 10.5%). The demand for laptops will shift further to the right than the demand for desktops.

The firm can use the YED estimate when **planning** changes in **output, employment and stocks**. When a product has a high income elasticity of demand, such as laptops, producers should be aware that demand will be highly sensitive to the living standards of consumers. In an **economic boom**, they can expect rising sales as demand shifts to the right but, in a **recession**, they should be prepared for falling demand and a fall in their **total revenue**.

The demand for **luxury boats** is likely to be more sensitive to the **economic cycle** than the demand for **basic foods** in supermarkets.

Cross-price elasticity of demand (XPED)	This is defined as the **responsiveness of demand for good X following changes in the price of a related good Y**. Cross Price Elasticity of Demand (XPED) $= \dfrac{\text{\% change in the demand for good X}}{\text{\% change in the price of good Y}}$ ● **XPED will be positive for substitute goods.** A rise in the price of local bus travel, which is a substitute for rail travel, should cause a rise in the demand for rail travel. When the substitutes are close substitutes, the value of XPED should be high. ● **XPED will be negative for complements.** A rise in the price of DVD players should cause a fall in demand not only for these products, but also for DVDs as the two goods are in joint demand. When the complements are closely related, the value of XPED should be high. ● **XPED will be zero** (or close to it) for completely unrelated goods.
Using cross price elasticity of demand	The firm can use a XPED estimate when **planning** changes in **output, employment and stocks** in response to changes in the price of substitutes or complements. When the product has a close substitute, such as a brand of washing powder, producers should be aware that demand will be highly sensitive to changes in the price of competing products. A rise in the price of a rival brand will cause a large outward shift in demand.
Price elasticity of supply (PES)	This is defined as the **responsiveness of quantity supplied to a change in the good's own price**. PES $= \dfrac{\text{\% change in the quantity supplied of good X}}{\text{\% change in the price of good X}}$
Diagrams for different PES values	*Figure 4.4(a)* *Figure 4.4(b)* *Figure 4.4(c)* 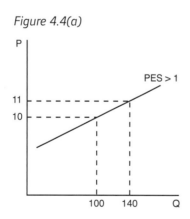 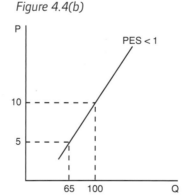 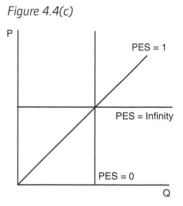

Figure 4.4 shows supply curves with different PES values. It is worth noting that any straight line supply curve that goes through the origin has unitary PES.

● **If the PES is greater than one, the good is elastic.** Supply is highly responsive to a change in price. A straight line supply curve that is elastic will cut the price axis (see Figure 4.4(a)). If the price rose from 10p to 11p, then the PES would be 4. The percentage change in quantity supplied is 40% while the percentage change in price is 10%.

● **If the PES is less than one, the good is inelastic.** Supply is not very responsive to changes in price. A straight line supply curve that is inelastic will cut the quantity axis (see Figure 4.4(b)). If the price fell from 10p to 5p, then the PES would be 0.7. The percentage change in quantity supplied is 35% while the percentage change in price is 50%.

● **If the PES is equal to 1, the good has unit elasticity.** The percentage change in quantity supplied is equal to the percentage change in price. Any straight line supply curve that originates from the origin has a PES of equal to one (see Figure 4.4(c)).

● **If the PES is equal to zero, the good is totally inelastic.** A change in price has no effect on the quantity supplied. The supply to the market is assumed to be fixed and will not change with price (see Figure 4.4(c)). A football stadium has a totally inelastic supply curve as the stadiums capacity cannot be changed even if there is massive demand from spectators to watch a match.

● **If the PES is infinity, the good is perfectly elastic.** Any change in price will see quantity supplied fall to zero (see Figure 4.4(c)).

Factors that influence PES

To understand whether supply is likely to be elastic, consider the following factors affecting whether firms can respond to price increases by expanding supply:

1. **Level of spare capacity** – if firms are working well below **full capacity** they can increase supply quickly and will have elastic supply curves. The higher the amount of spare capacity, the more elastic the supply. This is particularly relevant when an industry has experienced a downturn in demand leaving plenty of **under-utilised** productive resources.

2. **Substitutability of factors of production** – if factors of production can be easily moved into the production of a good or service, supply will be elastic. If resources used to make CD players were switched into the production of MP3 players, when demand for MP3 players increased then supply could have responded to meet the demand easily.

3. **Level of stocks and work in progress** – if firms have low levels of **stocks** (or **inventories**) they may not be able to respond quickly to changes in demand and will therefore have inelastic supply curves. In contrast, when a producer has a high level of unsold stocks they can supply extra output quickly to a market (although they may have to discount prices heavily to offload excess stock). This is sometimes seen in the car industry.

4. **Time period under consideration** – in the **short run**, at least one factor is assumed to be fixed. This will tend to limit the elasticity of supply. Supply will become more elastic in the **long run** when all factor inputs in the production process can be varied and a business can alter the scale of production to meet changing demand.

5. **Production lags** – in some industries there are clearly understood **production lags** where there is an inevitable time lag between using the factor inputs and the final product becoming available. This includes agricultural markets where supply cannot always respond elastically to fluctuations in demand. In the very short run the supply of products, such as cereals, may be perfectly inelastic.

Chapter 5

Unit 1: Introductory concepts → **Markets generally work well** → Sometimes markets fail → This may justify government intervention → Government failure sometimes occurs

The price mechanism

Competitive markets

A competitive market is one in which no individual supplier or consumer can influence the price. Instead, the price is set by the interaction of overall market supply and demand, to which consumers and firms respond. If there is an excess demand or supply at the current market price, this creates an incentive for participants in the market to change their behaviour. Thus **market forces** push the price towards an **equilibrium**, market clearing, level (as outlined in Chapter 3).

Allocative efficiency

Remember that the subject of Economics is concerned with the study of the allocation of scarce resources. An efficient resource allocation occurs when society's scarce resources are allocated between competing uses in such a way as the total **utility or satisfaction** derived from the resources is maximised.

The price mechanism and its functions

The price mechanism is the system by which changes in the relative prices of goods serve to allocate resources in a market economy. This occurs through the three functions of the price mechanism. Suppose that, with the market for a good initially in equilibrium, demand for the good then increases. The three functions would work in the following way:

Rationing function – In the first instance, the increase in demand for the good creates an excess demand for the product at the current price. Market forces will then cause the price to start rising; this rations the available supply of the product and those consumers willing to pay higher prices for it are those who purchase the good.

Signalling function – The rising price acts as a signal to producers that there is an excess demand for the product.

Incentive function – Because the higher price raises the profit margin on each unit of the good supplied, it creates an incentive for producers to expand supply. Resources are reallocated from other lines of production in order to expand supply of the product which has experienced a rise in demand.

In our example, the **price mechanism** has directed resources in line with consumer demand. This is sometimes known as **consumer sovereignty**. Demand comes from consumers who are assumed to be attempting to maximise their own utility. Thus the price mechanism has acted as an '**invisible hand**' (as described by Adam Smith) allocating resources in such a way to maximise utility or satisfaction.

Conditions for the price mechanism to achieve an efficient resource allocation

For the price mechanism to allocate resources efficiently, as outlined in the previous sub-section, a number of conditions must hold:

● Market participants must not be able to influence the price. This implies a **lack of monopoly power** on the part of suppliers. On the demand side, the equivalent concept is the absence of monopsony buying power.

● Market participants adopt **maximising behaviour** as outlined in Chapter 1. For example, consumers are selfish (acting to maximise their own utility or satisfaction) and **rational** (not making mistakes in maximising utility or satisfaction); firms act to maximise profits.

● There are no **externalities** (see Chapter 7) associated with the production or consumption of the product.

● **Perfect information** is available to all market participants. For example, consumers know about all the alternatives available for them when they spend their limited income.

● **Resources are perfectly mobile** between competing uses, so that they can be reallocated to other products when market forces cause changes in the relative prices of goods.

If these conditions are not satisfied, it is likely that **market failure** will result. It is also worth noting that an **efficient** resource allocation in no way implies that the outcome is **fair (equitable)**. A lack of equity is another possible source of market failure, although this concept is controversial because it is **normative** in nature.

Consumer surplus

The price that a consumer is willing to pay for a good reflects the utility or satisfaction that he or she derives from it. In competitive markets, there is a single market price paid by all consumers. Those who would, in fact, have been willing to pay more for the good if they had needed to receive a surplus.

Consumer surplus is the difference between what consumers are **willing** to pay for a good or service (indicated by the position of the demand curve) and what they **actually pay** (the market price).

Consumer surplus is shown in Figure 5.1 below.

Figure 5.1

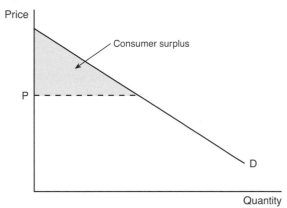

Changes in demand and consumer surplus

When there is a shift in the demand curve leading to a change in the equilibrium price and quantity traded, the amount of consumer surplus will alter.

This is shown in Figure 5.2. Following a shift in demand from D to D_1, the price rises to P_1 and quantity traded expands to Q_1. Consumer surplus was initially shown by the triangle AP_0B. This rises to area EP_1C.

Figure 5.2

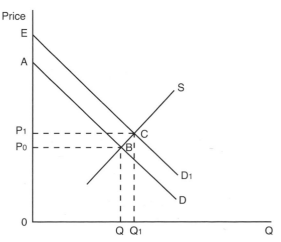

Producer surplus

Producer surplus is defined as the difference between what producers are willing and able to supply a good for (indicated by the position of the supply curve) and the price they actually receive.

Producer surplus is illustrated in Figure 5.3.

Figure 5.3

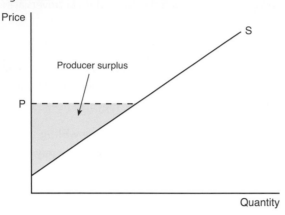

Relationships between goods

Sometimes two or more goods have special relationships in the price mechanism, so that a change in the market for one of the goods affects the market for another:

Substitutes – These are goods that are in **competitive demand** with one another, such as butter and margarine. A fall in the supply of butter will cause its price to rise and demand for it to contract. This serves to increase the demand for margarine (that is, to shift the demand curve to the right).

Complements – These are goods in **joint demand** such as dishwashers and dishwasher tablets. A fall in the supply of dishwashers would cause their price to rise and demand for them to contract. The demand for dishwasher tablets would then fall (shift to the left).

Joint supply – Some goods are by-products of other production processes. For example, bee keepers who produce honey are also able to supply beeswax for use on surfboards. An increase in the demand for honey causes its price to rise, leading to an extension of supply. This causes the supply of beeswax to increase (shift to the right).

Derived demand – The demand for some products is derived from the demand for others. For example, steel is rarely demanded for its own sake but for other uses such as construction. So the demand for steel is partly derived from the demand for buildings. When the supply of buildings increases, their price falls and demand expands. This then increases the demand for steel (demand shifts to the right). A common example of derived demand is that of labour, the demand for which is derived from the demand for the products and services that the workers produce.

Composite demand – Some goods are demanded for more than one purpose. Steel is needed not just for building but for making cars, for example. Its demand is composed of demand for these two uses and many others besides. If there is an increase in demand for steel for use in construction, this may reduce the supply of steel available to the car industry.

Chapter 6

Unit 1: Introductory concepts → Markets generally work well → **Sometimes markets fail** → This may justify government intervention → Government failure sometimes occurs

Market failure – Monopoly

Market failure

> **This box is repeated at the start of each chapter on market failure. You are recommended to read it each time.**
>
> When working well, competitive markets produce an efficient resource allocation through the price mechanism (see Chapter 5).
>
> **Market failure** refers to a situation in which markets produce undesirable outcomes. This can occur either in the form of **inefficient resource allocation** or a **lack of equity**.
>
> The main causes of market failure are: 1. Monopoly power; 2. Externalities; 3. Merit and demerit goods; 4. Public goods; 5. Imperfect information; 6. Resource immobility; 7. Unstable prices in commodity markets. The final source of market failure is different from the others, because it is normative in nature: 8. An unfair distribution of income (lack of equity).

Monopoly

Pure monopoly exists when there is a single supplier in a market. There are some pure monopolies, even though such situations are rare. Even powerful firms such as Microsoft do not enjoy a market share of 100%! As a result, the working definition of a monopolistic market relates to any firm with greater than 25% of the industry's total sales.

How do monopolies develop?

Monopoly power can be taken as the ability of the firm to influence its own price, rather than having it dictated by market forces. Monopolies can develop in the following ways:

- **Horizontal integration**

  Where two firms join at the same stage of production in the same industry. For example two car manufacturers merge, or a leading bank successfully takes over another bank.

- **Vertical integration**

  Where a firm develops market power by integrating with the different stages of production in an industry e.g. by buying its suppliers or controlling the main retail outlets. A good example is the oil industry where many of the leading companies are both producers and refiners of crude oil.

- **Creation of a statutory monopoly**

  Some key industries are given monopoly status. For example, water companies such as Severn Trent have a legally protected monopoly over the supply of domestic water and sewerage services.

- **Franchises and Licences**

  These give a firm the right to operate in a market – and are usually open to renewal every few years. Examples include:

  - Commercial radio licences
  - Commercial television
  - Local taxi route licences
  - Regional rail services
  - The National Lottery

- **Internal expansion of a firm**

  Firms can generate higher sales and increase market share by expanding their operations and exploiting possible economies of scale.

● **Branding**

When firms are able to **differentiate** their product from substitutes produced by other firms, this creates a basis for consumer loyalty, allowing firms to raise their prices while retaining some, or all, of their customers. **Consumer inertia** may also confer monopoly power. Gas suppliers, for example, may be able to retain customers after putting up their prices because of the effort involved for the consumer if they wish to switch providers.

To maintain a monopoly position, it is usually necessary that there are some entry barriers present. These are factors that make it costly or difficult for new firms to enter a market.

Monopolies and market failure

Where a single firm supplies the whole market, it is not subject to the competitive pressure of market forces. It can therefore set its own price, leading to a break down of the price mechanism. In order to raise the price, the monopolist must restrict the quantity (see the next sub-section and Figure 6.1). This means that fewer resources are allocated to this line of production than would have been the case if the price mechanism had directed resource allocation. These resources are now allocated to another use where they will not produce as much **utility or satisfaction**. As a result, a monopoly creates an **inefficient resource allocation** and is a source of market failure.

The monopolist is constrained by the demand curve

In the absence of government intervention, the only constraint on the ability of a monopoly to set its own price is the market demand curve, which shows the various price and quantity combinations that the market will support.

If the monopoly firm wishes to raise price above the level that would have prevailed in a competitive market, it must accept that demand will contract. Figure 6.1 shows this. The monopolist raises price from the competitive level of Pc to Pm. Demand contracts from Qc to Qm. There is not enough demand at price Pm to allow the monopolist to choose point X.

Figure 6.1

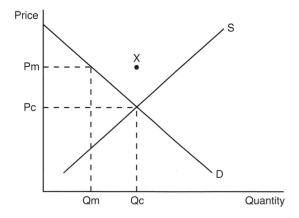

The damage caused by monopoly

The analysis above demonstrates that to use its price-making power to raise prices, the monopolist must accept that demand will contract (in other words, the monopolist must restrict supply to raise price).

The following analysis is not required by any of the exam boards at AS-level but can be very useful.

By raising price and restricting quantity, the monopoly reduces the level of consumer surplus compared to a competitive market. Some of the consumer surplus on the Qm units that are still sold (see Figure 6.2) is transferred to the monopoly firm as higher profit. However, the surplus that consumers previously enjoyed on the (Qc - Qm) units is lost. This is known as a **deadweight welfare loss** and is a measure of the damage caused by the inefficient resource allocation brought about by the monopoly.

Figure 6.2

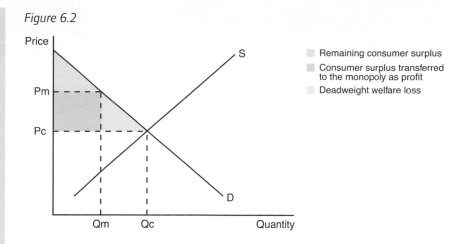

Price | S
Pm
Pc
D
Qm | Qc | Quantity

- Remaining consumer surplus
- Consumer surplus transferred to the monopoly as profit
- Deadweight welfare loss

Can monopoly be beneficial?

Possible benefits of monopoly include:

1. Monopoly profits may be reinvested into research and development. This may lead to the innovation of better products (enhancing the **dynamic efficiency** of the economy). Monopoly may also avoid **wasteful duplication** of research. However, a pure monopoly may fail to innovate due to the lack of competitive pressure.

2. Monopolies may lower costs of production by exploiting economies of scale that are not available to smaller firms (see Chapter 2).

3. Empirical evidence suggests that not all monopolies restrict supply and raise prices. Some firms in the real world sustain their power by selling high volumes of goods at low prices. Tesco and ToysRus are examples. This may actually increase consumer surplus and the welfare of consumers.

There are further benefits that may arise where firms have substantial market share without enjoying a pure monopoly:

4. The branding that firms use to win and protect market share can act as a guarantee of quality to the consumer.

5. Advertising expenditure undertaken in the pursuit of monopoly power may help fund television channels, newspapers, sports and community events, etc.

Monopoly profits may be used to produce the innovation of better products.

Chapter

7

Unit 1: Introductory concepts → Markets generally work well → **Sometimes markets fail** → This may justify government intervention → Government failure sometimes occurs

Market failure – externalities, merit and demerit goods and public goods

Market failure

> This box is repeated at the start of each chapter on market failure.
> You are recommended to read it each time.

When working well, competitive markets produce an efficient resource allocation through the price mechanism (see Chapter 5).

Market failure refers to a situation in which markets produce undesirable outcomes. This can occur either in the form of **inefficient resource allocation** or a **lack of equity**.

The main causes of market failure are: 1. Monopoly power; 2. Externalities; 3. Merit and demerit goods; 4. Public goods; 5. Imperfect information; 6. Resource immobility; 7. Unstable prices in commodity markets. The final source of market failure is different from the others, because it is normative in nature: 8. An unfair distribution of income (lack of equity).

Externalities

Externalities are defined as **third party** (or spill over) effects arising from the production or consumption of goods and services for which **no appropriate compensation** is paid (in other words, the effects are external to the market).

Positive externalities (external benefits) include the **third party** benefits arising from the production or consumption of goods and services. A good example is the external benefits of health care. While the individual who is treated gains a private benefit, treatment may also make him a more productive worker, benefiting his employer and generating tax revenue. The family and friends of those who are treated benefit, while those treated for contagious diseases do not pass their illness on to others.

Negative externalities are defined as **third party** costs arising from the production or consumption of goods and services. A good example is the external costs created by motoring. These include the emission of greenhouse gases such as carbon dioxide. Rational, self-interested, utility maximising consumers and profit making firms do not take into account the effects of their activities on third parties. **Market failure** is therefore likely to occur when externalities are present.

Social costs and benefits

The full social cost or social benefit of an activity takes account of the effects of the activity on third parties:

Social cost = Private cost + External cost

Social benefit = Private benefit + External benefit

It is clear that externalities create a divergence between private and social costs and between private and social benefits. Because market transactions only reflect private costs and benefits, markets will fail to produce an optimal resource allocation from society's perspective when externalities are present.

Example: Private and external costs and benefits of car ownership

Private costs	**Private Benefits**
● Road taxes	● Satisfaction of running a privately owned car
● Insurance	● Increased mobility and flexibility of lifestyle
● Running costs: maintenance; fuel and depreciation	● Convenience

External costs of car ownership

- Traffic congestion reduces average speeds and lengthens journey times.

- Slower journeys increase transportation costs for goods and services and add to the overall cost of living in the economy. This makes domestic firms less competitive.

- High accident rates in areas with congested traffic impose extra costs on the National Health Service. Another major problem is air pollution, which causes asthma and heart attacks.

External benefits of car ownership

- Output of the motor car industry generates employment and income in the economy.

- The motor car industry creates hundreds of thousands of jobs in related **complementary industries**:
    - Vehicle insurance
    - Repair and maintenance
    - Petrol Retailing
    - Design industries

- High levels of tax on petrol bring in very large amounts of tax revenue for the Treasury each year.

Merit goods

Merit goods are defined as goods that are **under provided** in a market economy. The price mechanism allocates fewer resources to their production than is thought socially desirable.

The best known examples of merit goods are education and healthcare, which would be very substantially under provided in a pure free market economy because the **social benefits are greater than the private benefits**.

There are a number of reasons why education would be under provided in a free market economy:

- The external benefits of education would not be taken into account by individuals deciding whether to pay for schooling. The **social benefit of education exceeds the private benefit**.

- Individuals might underestimate the private benefits of education (for example, the benefit of higher earnings potential). This is an example of **imperfect information** affecting the ability of the price mechanism to allocate resources efficiently.

Education is a merit good which would be substantially under provided in a pure free market economy.

● Even if individuals judge the private benefits correctly, they might **discount** them (place less weight on them) because the benefits occur largely in the future, rather than when the education is paid for.

● Those paying for education are rarely the direct recipient of its benefits. Education would usually be paid for by parents rather than by students.

All these factors may serve to reduce demand below the levels that are socially desirable. In the end, because social costs and benefits are not easy to measure, the judgement that a good is a merit good becomes a matter of opinion (a value judgement), introducing a normative element to the analysis.

Demerit goods

Demerit goods are defined as goods that are **over provided** in the market economy. The price mechanism allocates more resources to their production than is thought socially desirable.

Examples of demerit goods include cigarettes, alcohol and drugs.

Consumption of these goods generates negative externalities, so that the **social cost of consumption exceeds the private costs**. Of course, these negative externalities are not accounted for by the price mechanism.

Just as with merit goods, there are problems of imperfect information associated with demerit goods. There is a danger of smoking leading to lung cancer, for example, but no individual knows whether he/she will get lung cancer until it happens. Individuals may underestimate the risk and place little weight on it because of the fact that if it happens at all it is likely to occur some way in the future. Individuals tend to underestimate the private costs of consuming demerit goods.

Marginal analysis of merit and demerit goods

Marginal means 'one extra' or 'a little extra', thus the marginal benefit from a good is the benefit gained from one extra unit of consumption. Marginal concepts are important to economists, but they tend not to be examined at AS Level, being reserved instead for A2. However, the **AQA specification does** require that AS Level students be familiar with marginal analysis in relation to merit and demerit goods.

The starting point here is to understand that:

● **Marginal private benefit** (MPB) is the benefit to the individual of consuming the last unit of a good. This is effectively the demand curve for a good.

● **Marginal private cost** (MPC) is the cost to a firm of producing the last unit of a good. This is effectively the supply curve for a good.

● **Marginal social benefit** (MSB) is the benefit to the individual consuming the good, plus the external benefit, of the last unit of the good.

● **Marginal social cost** (MSC) is the cost to the firm, plus the external cost, of producing the last unit of a good.

Merit goods

Where substantial positive externalities exist, merit goods may be **under consumed or under provided** since the free market may fail to take into account the external benefits. This is because the **marginal social benefits** of consuming the good are **greater than the marginal private benefits**.

An example of positive externalities arising from the consumption of higher education is shown in Figure 7.1. In the example a consumer benefits privately from higher education that also creates external benefits such as increases in productivity. Thus MSB is higher than MPB.

A market failure problem is likely to exist because the benefit to society in terms of higher productivity and a higher GDP is unpriced by the price mechanism. This leads to the **privately optimal level of output being less than the socially optimal level of production**.

Figure 7.1

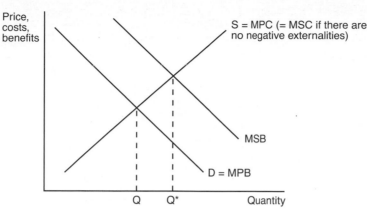

The consumer simply does not take into account the external benefits of higher education. The private optimum occurs where the marginal private benefit (the benefit to the individual of consuming the last unit) equals marginal private cost, giving an output of **Q**. At this level of output, the distance between the MPB and the MSB represents the size of the external benefit.

If we assume that there are no negative externalities, then MPC will equal the MSC. In terms of social efficiency, education is under consumed. The socially optimal level of output is where MSB = MSC, giving output of **Q***. The under provision of the merit good is shown as Q* - Q. Society as a whole could be made better off by increasing the current level of output from Q to Q*.

Demerit goods

For demerit goods, negative externalities create a divergence between private costs and social costs. When negative externalities exist, **marginal social cost > marginal private cost**. A profit maximising firm will **ignore these external costs** when determining its price and output strategy and focus purely on the private costs and benefits.

Consider the following example of a firm producing negative externalities. A chemical factory discharges its waste products into a local river. This **kills off the fish stock** and causes **illness** amongst water sports' enthusiasts who use the river for recreational purposes.

A market failure problem is likely to exist because the cost to society in terms of the deterioration of the environment is unpriced by the price mechanism. This leads to the **privately optimal level of output being greater than the socially optimal level of production**. This is illustrated in Figure 7.2.

Figure 7.2

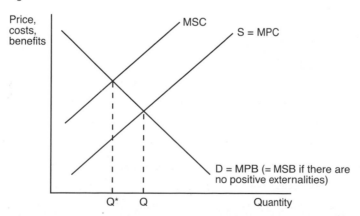

The **private optimum** occurs where the **marginal private benefit equals the marginal private cost**, giving an output of **Q**. At this level of output, the distance between the MPC and the MSC represents the size of the external costs that are ignored by the producer.

Public goods include flood control systems such as the Thames Barrier.

If we assume that there are no positive externalities then marginal private benefit will be equal to marginal social benefit. The socially optimal level of output in this industry occurs, where MSB = MSC. At Q*, the effects of chemical production on the environment are considered. The over provision of the demerit good is shown as Q-Q*. Society as a whole could be made better off by reducing the current level of output from Q to Q*.

Public goods

Public goods are defined in terms of two key characteristics:

● **Non-excludability** – consumption of the good cannot be confined to those who have paid for it.

● **Non-rivalry in consumption** – the consumption by one individual does not reduce the availability of goods to others.

Examples of public goods include flood control systems, street lighting and national defence. A flood control system, such as the Thames Barrier, cannot be confined to those who have paid for the service. Also the consumption of the service by one household will not reduce its availability to others.

Most goods are **private goods**, which are excludable (you only get the good if you pay for it).

No consumer would pay for a public good that could be consumed for free if another household decided to purchase it. This is the **free-rider problem**. As a result, no public goods would be provided if it were left to the private sector. This is why governments intervene to ensure that resources are allocated to the production of public goods.

Note that this market failure is slightly different in one respect from the others. The market for public goods may be **missing** from the price mechanism, because public goods might not be provided by the private sector at all. This in contrast to other goods where the market is present but fails to achieve an efficient allocation of resources.

Quasi-public goods are products that are public in nature, but do not exhibit fully the features of non-excludability and non-rivalry. The road network in the UK is currently available to all, but could be made excludable via a system of tolls. There is also non-rivalry in consumption, but only up to an extent. Once the road becomes congested there is rivalry in consumption.

Market failure

> This box is repeated at the start of each chapter on market failure.
> You are recommended to read it each time.

> When working well, competitive markets produce an efficient resource allocation through the price mechanism (see Chapter 5).
>
> **Market failure** refers to a situation in which markets produce undesirable outcomes. This can occur either in the form of **inefficient resource allocation** or a **lack of equity**.
>
> The main causes of market failure are: 1. Monopoly power; 2. Externalities; 3. Merit and demerit goods; 4. Public goods; 5. Imperfect information; 6. Resource immobility; 7. Unstable prices in commodity markets. The final source of market failure is different from the others, because it is normative in nature: 8. An unfair distribution of income (lack of equity).

Imperfect information

Chapter 5 showed that the price mechanism will only allocate resources efficiently if market participants enjoy perfect information.

The price mechanism allows resources to follow consumer demand, but the result only maximises utility (satisfaction) on the assumption that consumers are rational, self-interested utility maximisers and that they have the correct information on which to base their decisions.

Suppose a consumer is choosing a flat screen television with a budget of £600. There are huge numbers of different products available. It is unlikely that a consumer will choose the one that maximises their utility unless they have information on a wide range of different televisions. The consumer would need to research information on the features of each television. These might include screen size, picture sharpness, connectivity to other devices, range of viewing angles and many others besides.

Similarly, firms must have full information, for example about the profit margins available to them in other lines of production. If this is not the case, firms cannot respond appropriately to the signals and incentives provided by the price mechanism.

Symmetric information refers to a situation where the buyer and seller of the product have the same information.

Asymmetric information occurs when either the buyer or seller possess more information than the other party.

Asymmetric information is a particular example of the problem of imperfect information. George Akerlof brought the issue to prominence when writing about the *Market for Lemons*, a lemon being a low quality second hand car, while a high quality car is a peach. The seller of a second hand car is likely to know whether it is a lemon or a peach, the buyer, however, has no way of telling. This could lead to a buyer mistakenly paying an excessive price for a lemon. Moreover, given the uncertainty, he/she is likely to be unwilling to pay the appropriate price for a high quality car (peach). This means that sellers are unlikely to bring peaches to market, because they will not be paid full value for them: it would seem that there cannot be an efficient market in high quality used cars!

Of course, there are ways in which sellers can attempt to **signal** the high quality of their 'peach', for example by maintaining a full service history. Buyers can protect themselves by paying for a mechanic to inspect the car before they buy. However, these practices themselves are an additional cost to those concerned arising from the **asymmetric information problem**.

Examples of asymmetric information are widespread. They include:

● Mechanics possessing specialist information about service and maintenance of cars, but this information is not known by the customer.

● Employers attempting to judge the quality of job applicants through an application form, references and a short interview. However, the applicant is likely to be better informed about his skills and personality than the firm that is considering hiring him.

● Sellers of houses covering up problems such as damp, cracks in walls and stains in carpets to hide them from prospective buyers.

● Those purchasing goods on e-Bay without actually seeing them, whereas the seller has a more complete knowledge of the product they are selling.

Factor of production (resource) immobility

The signals of the price mechanism change when costs of production or patterns of consumer demand change. This requires resources to be reallocated, but some resources are not mobile between uses and this results in market failure in two main ways:

● **The market may not be able to respond to changes in consumer demand.** Suppose consumer demand shifted massively from Good A to Good B, for example. The market may not be able to respond to this change if the resources (land, labour, capital and enterprise) used in producing Good A could not be switched to producing Good B.

● **Resources may become unemployed if they are no longer in demand for their current use and cannot be transferred to other uses.** This is called structural unemployment. When demand for UK coal fell in the 1980s many miners were structurally unemployed as they lacked skills to work in other areas of the economy.

Unstable prices in commodity markets

Commodities are homogeneous products or materials such as agricultural produce (e.g. wheat, rice, coffee, cocoa beans), metals (e.g. copper and steel) and fuels (e.g. oil). There tends to be a single global price for commodities, determined by the forces of supply and demand.

Commodity markets are notorious for exhibiting price volatility. Prices on commodity markets fluctuate hour-by-hour and minute-by-minute and there can be periods of sharp price rises and falls. Such price volatility creates uncertainty (an example of imperfect information). This is not efficient and therefore can be considered a source of market failure. Think about the broader economic effects of sharp swings in oil prices to see why this is so.

Reasons for unstable prices commodity prices

1. Supply of agricultural commodities is often affected by factors beyond human control, such as weather and disease. Sudden shortages or gluts of produce result in price swings. See Figure 8.1.

2. Supply of commodities is often **inelastic** in the short term. This magnifies the effect on prices of changes in demand. See Figure 8.2.

3. Demand for some commodities can change arbitrarily. A cold winter can significantly increase the demand for oil, for example.

4. Commodities are often traded for **speculative reasons**. An expectation of price rises may cause increased demand from those hoping to make a capital gain, and this may exacerbate the extent of the price rises.

Figure 8.1: The market for coffee beans (1)

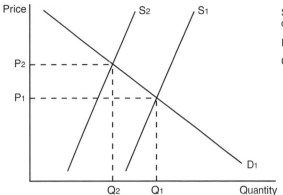

Supply shifts from S1 to S2 (for example, due to frost in Brazil affecting coffee crops).

Price rises from P1 to P2.

Quantity traded falls from Q1 to Q2.

Figure 8.2: The market for coffee beans (2)

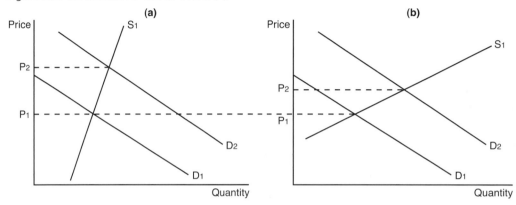

Demand increases from D1 to D2, for example because of a change in tastes towards coffee rather than tea, or because of speculative activity.

The supply of coffee beans is relatively inelastic in the short run, as in part (a) of the diagram. The resulting price increase from P1 to P2 is bigger than it would have been if supply had been more elastic as in part (b) of the diagram.

Many commodities are processed into final products. For example, coffee beans are ground and processed to make instant coffee. The prices of final products tend to be more stable than commodity prices. Taking instant coffee as an example, reasons for this include:

- Coffee beans are only a fraction of the overall costs of producing instant coffee.

- Producers of instant coffee may hold substantial stocks of beans and therefore may not be affected immediately by price fluctuations.

- Producers can insure themselves against fluctuating bean prices by taking out 'futures contracts'. These contracts guarantee the delivery of beans in the future at a price agreed today.

- Even if affected by fluctuating prices for beans, frequently changing prices for the instant coffee produced from them would carry a significant cost to producers.

A lack of equity (fairness)

The final cause of market failure is different in nature from all the others. This is why this section of text has been highlighted. The others have all been about inefficiency of resource allocation (a positive economic concept). However, many people consider that markets produce unfair outcomes and that this is also a market failure. This is a normative perspective.

Consider, for example, the distribution of income, which is largely determined in labour markets. It might be considered unfair that the top 20% of income earners enjoy as much as 50% of the national income. If so, this lack of equity constitutes a market failure and would justify government intervention to make the distribution of income more equal.

Chapter

9

Unit 1: Introductory concepts → Markets generally work well → Sometimes markets fail → **This may justify government intervention** → **Government failure sometimes occurs**

Government intervention – indirect taxation, subsidies, state provision, price controls, buffer stocks

Government intervention

This box is repeated at the start of each chapter on government intervention. You are recommended to read it each time.

Government intervention is used to correct market failures arising from an inefficient resource allocation or a lack of equity.

The main forms of government intervention are: 1.Indirect taxation; 2. Subsidies; 3. State provision; 4. Price controls; 5. Buffer stocks; 6. Regulation; 7. Pollution permits; 8. Extensions of property rights.

Government intervention will not necessarily be **effective** in achieving its aims or succeed in improving the **efficiency** of resource allocation or improving **equity**.

Indirect taxation (tackling market failures associated with negative externalities and demerit goods)

Indirect taxes are a tax on expenditure imposed by the government on producers. Indirect taxes are most likely to be used to reduce the number of resources allocated to the product and therefore can be used to tackle problems associated with negative externalities and demerit goods.

Indirect taxes raise a firm's costs and therefore cause an upward shift in the firm's supply curve. This means that less can be supplied at each price. A **unit tax** (or **specific tax**) will cause a **parallel shift** in the supply curve and is illustrated in Figure 9.1. The vertical distance between the supply curves shows the amount of tax per unit.

Figure 9.1

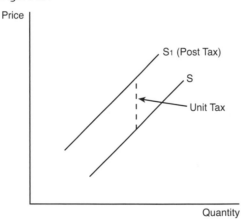

Figure 9.2

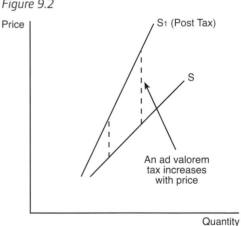

An **ad valorem** (**percentage tax**) will cause the supply curve to **tilt to the left**. This is because the size of the tax increases with price. This is illustrated in Figure 9.2. For example a 17.5% tax on £1 is 17.5p, much smaller than the same tax of £17.50 on £100.

The effects of indirect taxation on consumers and producers are dependent on the price elasticity of demand.

● In Figure 9.3 demand is **relatively price inelastic**. The producer finds it easier to pass on the tax to the consumer. The total tax per unit is ac, but the consumer pays the majority of the tax (ab) while the producer burden is bc. The quantity produced in equilibrium contracts from Q to Q_1. Total tax revenue = tax per unit (ac) x quantity traded (Q_1), and is represented by the shaded area.

Figure 9.3

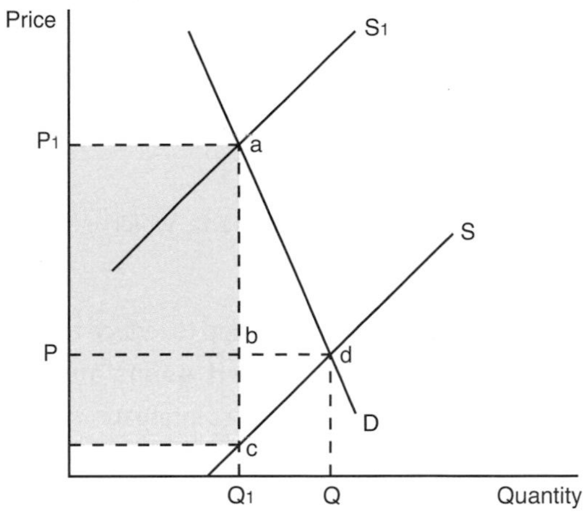

Figure 9.4

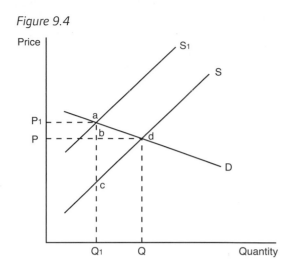

- In Figure 9.4 demand is **relatively price elastic**. The producer finds it difficult to pass on the tax to the consumer and has to **absorb** the majority of the tax itself. The producer burden (bc) outweighs the consumer burden (ab). There is a larger contraction in the quantity bought and sold – with the equilibrium quantity falling from Q to Q₁.

- When demand is inelastic the consumer faces a large price rise and, as a result, the fall in **consumer surplus** (PP₁ad) is greater than when demand is inelastic. A fall in consumer surplus will reduce consumer welfare.

Evaluating indirect taxes in tackling demerit goods

One of the most common policies used to tackle the problems created by demerit goods is the introduction of an indirect tax. The aim of an indirect tax is to **increase the firm's costs** so that the firm is forced to take into account the external costs that it generates. It will result in a lower level of output and a more efficient allocation of resources. Examples of such taxes include: petrol tax, vehicle excise duty, landfill tax and the carbon tax.

There are however some problems in using indirect taxes to tackle the problems created by demerit goods:

- Negative externalities are difficult to measure and, as a result, setting the indirect tax at the correct level is virtually impossible. In reality, therefore, all that governments and regulatory agencies can hope to achieve is a movement towards a more efficient allocation of resources.

- Indirect taxes **reduce output and raise prices**, and this will have an adverse effect on consumer welfare.

- If the aim of indirect taxation is to discourage activities that generate negative externalities, or to reduce consumption of demerit goods, the effectiveness of the policy will be reduced if demand is **inelastic**. This is a concern because there are good reasons in theory to expect demand for many demerit goods such as cigarettes and alcohol (addictive nature) and petrol (a near necessity for many aspects of modern living) to be inelastic.

- Taxes on some demerit goods may have a **regressive** effect (see Chapter 24) making the distribution of income less equal.

- If indirect taxes are raised in one country to tackle pollution, producers may shift production to countries with lower taxes. This will not reduce global pollution, and may create problems such as **unemployment and a lack of competitiveness** in the country that raised the tax.

- There may be more effective ways of improving the efficiency of resource allocation in relation to demerit goods. The effectiveness of indirect taxes should be compared against alternatives such as regulation or educating consumers about the private costs of consuming demerit goods such as cigarettes and alcohol.

● One advantage of indirect taxes is that they raise substantial revenue for the government and help fund public services.

Subsidies
(tackling market failures associated with positive externalities and merit goods)

Subsidies are **payments** made to producers by the government, which effectively reduce costs and encourage them to increase output.

The effect of a subsidy is to increase the quantity of goods sold and to reduce the market equilibrium price. Government subsidies are often offered to producers of **merit goods and services** such as public transport and industries requiring some **protection** from low cost international competition.

Figure 9.5

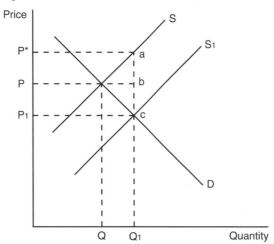

● Figure 9.5 shows a specific subsidy equal to ac per unit produced.

● The subsidy causes the firm's supply curve to shift to the right because the firm's costs are reduced.

● The total amount spent by the government on the subsidy is equal to the unit subsidy (ac) x Q_1. This is equal to the area P_1P^*ac. The consumer gain is equal to the distance (bc) while the producer gain is equal to (ab).

● The more inelastic the demand curve, the greater the fall in prices and the consumer's gain from a subsidy. Indeed when demand is totally inelastic the consumer gains the entire subsidy (but consumption does not increase at all).

Evaluating subsidies

● By increasing consumption of goods associated with positive externalities and merit goods, a subsidy may help improve **the efficiency of resource allocation**.

● The effectiveness of a subsidy in increasing consumption of a product depends on the elasticity of demand. The effectiveness of the policy is increased if demand is elastic.

● There is a danger that subsidies may support firms that are **inefficient and wasteful** in their production processes. Such firms might not survive in highly competitive markets without government support.

● Government subsidies carry an expense to the taxpayer. There is an **opportunity cost** here: the money could have been put to other uses. To spend the money on a subsidy is only sensible if it is the best use for the money.

State provision

(tackling market failures associated with merit goods and public goods)

In some cases, rather than subsidising goods, the state pays for them entirely, making them free of charge. Examples include merit goods such as education and healthcare (most NHS treatment is free of charge to patients, although there are some exceptions such as prescription charges). Public goods such as national defence and street lighting are also provided by the state.

Evaluating state provision

The points already made in relation to evaluating subsidies apply also to evaluating state provision. Note too:

● The cost of state provision is especially expensive because the good is subsidised to the point at which it is actually free of charge. Consider the huge annual cost of the NHS, for example.

● The danger of inefficient production and waste is enhanced in government run organisations, because of the lack of a profit motive.

● Governments may attempt to reduce the risk of inefficiency by financing the good free of charge to consumers and paying private sector firms to produce the service. Schools could be run by private companies, for example, in return for payment from the state. Those companies who became more efficient would increase the profits they made from the money paid to them by the government. There would be dangers, however: a drive for efficiency may reduce quality. The government would have to allocate resources to monitoring and regulating the performance of private firms running schools.

● The effectiveness of state provision in increasing consumption is likely to be limited only by the resources available. When a good or service is free of charge, economic theory suggests that any consumer who gets any utility from it at all will choose to use it. Figure 9.6 could represent the NHS. There is an excess demand for treatment and because the price is set at zero, the rationing function of prices has been suppressed. Some other way must be found of rationing available treatments. This may be 'first come first served' (NHS waiting lists!), prioritising on the basis of who needs treatment most or even the luck of the draw (the treatments available on the NHS differ in different parts of the country – the 'postcode lottery'!)

Figure 9.6

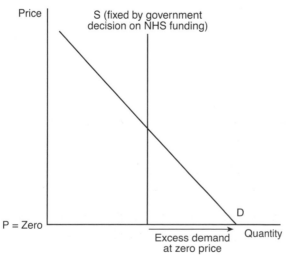

Chapter

10

Unit 1: Introductory concepts → Markets generally work well → Sometimes markets fail
→ **This may justify government intervention** → **Government failure sometimes occurs**

Government intervention – price controls, buffer stocks

Government intervention

> **This box is repeated at the start of each chapter on government intervention. You are recommended to read it each time.**
>
> Government intervention is used to correct market failures arising from an inefficient resource allocation or a lack of equity.
>
> The main forms of government intervention are: 1.Indirect taxation; 2. Subsidies; 3. State provision; 4. Price controls; 5. Buffer stocks; 6. Regulation; 7. Pollution permits; 8. Extensions of property rights.
>
> Government intervention will not necessarily be **effective** in achieving its aims or succeed in improving the **efficiency** of resource allocation or improving **equity**.

Price controls

Governments can intervene to impose legally binding price controls on a market, in the form of a maximum or minimum price.

Maximum prices

(tackling a lack of equity for consumers)

A maximum price is a **price ceiling**. To be effective, it must be set below the market equilibrium. A maximum price set above the equilibrium has no effect on the market.

A maximum price might be used to tackle a market failure arising from a lack of equity. It might be considered unfair that some goods are not sufficiently affordable to consumers. Indeed, some **firms** voluntarily set maximum prices for their products for this reason. The price for sell out sports fixtures and concerts is below the equilibrium. Part of the reason for this is the **equity** consideration of ensuring that fans are not priced out of the market by corporate hospitality and the rich.

Figure 10.1 shows a maximum price. Because the price ceiling is set at P_1, there will be a contraction of market supply and expansion of market demand leading to a shortage (**excess demand**) in the market equal to Q_1-Q_2.

Figure 10.1

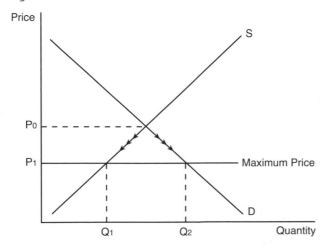

Evaluating maximum prices

The excess demand created by a maximum price cannot be cleared because the **rationing function** (see Chapter 5) of prices has been suppressed. This means that there must be some other way of rationing the product. Options include:

1. 'First come first served' (queuing). This is a particularly inefficient option, taking up the time of people stuck in the queue. Consider traffic jams, caused by queues for road space!

2. Seller's preference (the seller chooses to whom they sell the product, for example loyal customers).

3. Lucky ballot (random selection of who gets to buy the product).

● It is a **normative** (subjective opinion) based consideration as to whether a maximum price improves fairness. However, it might be noted that the excess demand means that some people who are willing to pay for the product are not able to make a purchase.

● It may prove difficult to suppress the functioning of the free market and it is possible that the shortage may lead to a black market developing. This means that the product may still be rationed by price to an extent, with those willing to pay more receiving the good.

● Thus, to make a maximum price scheme effective, the authorities must spend resources to discourage **black markets** (detecting and punishing those who purchase at the maximum price to sell on to others at a profit).

Minimum prices
(tackling a lack of equity for suppliers)

A minimum price is a **price floor**. To be effective it must be set above the market equilibrium. A minimum price set below the equilibrium has no effect on the market.

The reason for setting a minimum price would normally be to ensure that suppliers receive what is considered to be a fair price, thus guaranteeing them a decent standard of living. Minimum prices are common in agriculture. The national minimum wage is another well known example of a minimum price.

Figure 10.2 shows a minimum price. If the minimum price is set at P_1, there will be an excess supply equal to Q_2-Q_1. This is because the above equilibrium price causes demand to contract and supply to expand.

Figure 10.2

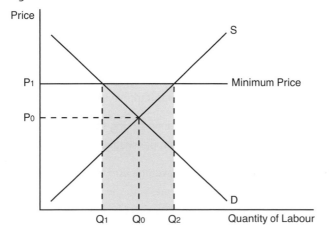

Evaluating minimum prices

● It is a **normative** consideration as to whether any particular minimum price improves fairness. Note, however, that consumers pay higher prices than they would in the absence of government intervention.

● The minimum price may be influenced by political pressure on the part of producers who stand to benefit from higher prices. This may create conflict between political and economic objectives, a potential source of **government failure** (see Chapter 12).

● To maintain a minimum price it is likely that the governing authorities will have to buy up the excess supply at the agreed minimum price (this is called **intervention buying**). The cost of doing this is represented by the shaded area in Figure 10.2. This expense carries an opportunity cost, as the money could have been spent on other projects. Might some of these projects have been a better use of the money?

● Once purchased, the excess supply is likely to be destroyed. This constitutes a waste of scarce resources. It would be more efficient to pay producers to do nothing than to use resources to produce output that will be destroyed!

Buffer stocks
(tackling market failure due to price instability in commodity markets)

A buffer stock is used to stabilise prices of a product in the face of fluctuating supply and to prevent the periodic shortages that are seen in many commodity markets.

Figure 10.3 illustrates the working of a buffer stock scheme. Many commodities have inelastic supply in the short run, and the diagram assumes for simplicity that supply is totally inelastic.

In periods of high supply (see S_1 in Figure 10.3) the government engages in intervention buying (quantity bc) to maintain the target price. This supply is stored, and is released back onto the market if needed at a later date. In periods of shortage (S_2) quantity ab is released from the buffer stock, thereby preventing prices from rising.

Figure 10.3

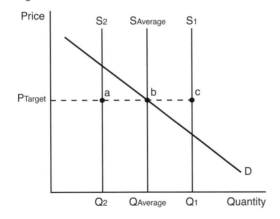

Evaluating buffer stocks

● Buffer stocks can in theory be self-financing. If the price is set at the long run average, the money spent on intervention buying during periods of surplus is recovered when the buffer stock is released at a later date. The **stabilisation** of the price helps improve efficiency.

● However, the above point ignores the costs of administering the scheme and storing the buffer stock. Also, there may be waste as some commodities are perishable and cannot be stored indefinitely.

● The target price is often set above the long run average due to political pressure from producers. This makes the scheme in effect a minimum price scheme, with the expense and waste that this might imply, while raising questions about **equity**, because consumers face higher prices.

● Buffer stocks may struggle to stabilise the price if any major producers are not part of the scheme. During periods of surplus, other producers are likely to undercut the target price of the buffer stock scheme.

● Empirical evidence suggests that buffer stocks have often not been effective in stabilising prices.

Chapter

11

Unit 1: Introductory concepts → Markets generally work well → Sometimes markets fail → **This may justify government intervention** → **Government failure sometimes occurs**

Government intervention – regulation, extension of property rights, pollution permits

Government intervention

> This box is repeated at the start of each chapter on government intervention. You are recommended to read it each time.

> Government intervention is used to correct market failures arising from an inefficient resource allocation or a lack of equity.
>
> The main forms of government intervention are: 1. Indirect taxation; 2. Subsidies; 3. State provision; 4. Price controls; 5. Buffer stocks; 6. Regulation; 7. Pollution permits; 8. Extensions of property rights.
>
> Government intervention will not necessarily be **effective** in achieving its aims or succeed in improving the **efficiency** of resource allocation or improving **equity**.

Regulation
(tackling the market failures of monopoly power, negative externalities and demerit goods)

Governments sometimes seek to tackle market failures by putting into place legal restrictions (regulations) on the behaviour of firms and consumers. For example:

Regulating monopoly power

● In the UK, the Competition Commission is empowered to investigate mergers and takeovers and block them if they think the mergers and takeovers will result in excessive monopoly power.

● The Office of Fair Trading investigates and remedies anti-competitive practices such as cartels and other price fixing agreements. Firms can be fined up to 10% of turn over and company directors jailed for price fixing.

● Permanent regulatory bodies oversee the conduct of firms providing household utilities such as water, gas and electricity. For example, OFWAT has the power to cap the prices charged by the regional water monopolies.

Regulating demerit goods

● Some drugs are illegal.

● There are age restrictions on who can buy alcohol and cigarettes.

● Smoking is not allowed in enclosed public spaces.

Regulating negative externalities (such as pollution)

● The enforcement of minimum environmental standards is common in many industries, in order to protect air and water quality and restrict emissions of green house gases.

● Firms can be fined if their production processes emit pollution in excess of the legally permitted levels.

Evaluating regulation

- Regulations must be enforced and this carries an **administrative cost**. There is an opportunity cost in devoting scarce resources to the process of regulation. High administrative costs are a potential source of **government failure** (see Chapter 12), as is the next issue, a lack of information.

- The success of regulation depends partly on the quality of information available to regulators. For example, it is difficult to judge the optimal levels of pollution because it is difficult to place a monetary value on negative externalities. A further example is that utility regulators attempt to set the price much as it would be in a competitive market, but may lack the information to judge this accurately.

- Note the optimal level of pollution is unlikely to be zero, because this would imply zero economic activity.

- Regulation of negative externalities in production attempts to force all firms to cut their emissions to the legally allowed level. Some firms will find it very costly (**inefficient**) to do so, but the law will still attempt to enforce this.

- There may be superior policies available. For example, in the field of negative externalities, the policies of **extending property rights** and allocating **tradable pollution permits** are highly regarded. **Negative externalities** could also be tackled by indirect taxation.

Extending property rights
(tackling market failure associated with negative externalities in production)

Negative externalities arise largely from the fact that nobody owns the environment and it is therefore free to use.

Consider the example of a chemical factory that discharges its waste products into a local river. This kills some fish, negatively affecting third parties in the form of the local fishing club who use the river.

Allocating ownership of the river to the fishing club would produce an efficient outcome. Where the benefit to the chemical company of polluting the river exceeded the cost to the fishing club of allowing that pollution, the chemical company would be able to compensate the fishing club and both parties would be better off. This would work the other way round if ownership of the river was given to the chemical firm. In either case, all mutually beneficial trades would be undertaken and the socially optimal level of pollution found.

Evaluating the extension of property rights

- The extension of property rights is a theoretically simple method of achieving an efficient economic outcome, as analysed above.

- The externality is successfully **internalised** (brought back within the market system). If the fishing club own the river, the chemical company is forced to pay for the pollution it generates.

- There is no need for regulatory authorities to try to make artificial judgements about the optimal level of pollution.

- For these reasons, extending property rights is often thought to be an effective and superior alternative to regulating pollution.

- However, it will be necessary to legally protect the property rights of the owners of environmental resources. This itself carries a cost and may be difficult (could the polluting activities of the chemical company be accurately measured and checked against levels that have been agreed with the fishing club?)

- There are **equity** considerations. The optimal level of pollution will be found regardless of who is allocated ownership of the river, but this decision affects the **distribution of income and wealth**: you are better off if you own something than if you don't. An option is for the government to auction the property rights in the first instance, thereby generating revenue.

Regulation of negative externalities in production attempts to force all firms to cut their emissions to the legally allowed level.

Marketable pollution permits

An alternative to full allocation of property rights is for governments to cap pollution at what they judge to be the optimal level. Firms are then allocated permits to allow them to emit a certain level of pollution in an agreed time period (say a year) but can sell any permits that they do not need to other firms. Such **'emissions trading'** or **'cap and trade'** schemes have become increasingly prominent and have been extended to international agreements, where countries have permits to produce agreed levels of pollution but can sell these permits to other countries if they wish.

Evaluating marketable pollution permits

● The key advantage of pollution permits is that those firms or countries who find it least costly to control pollution will do so and then sell their spare permits to those who find it most expensive. The most efficient way of reaching the desired level of pollution is therefore found.

● International cap and trade schemes can be used to address injustices in the international distribution of income. If poor countries are allocated sufficient permits, they can sell them to richer countries who wish to carry on polluting. The effect is that the richer countries compensate the poorer for the pollution generated.

● As with the allocation of property rights, what was previously an externality (outside the market) has been **internalised** and those who pollute now have to pay for their activities.

● However, the scheme does require a judgement to be reached about the optimal level of pollution. Such a judgement is incredibly difficult to make.

● A new market in pollution permits has been created and this market itself may be subject to **market failures**.

● The trading of permits affects the geographical distribution of pollution. Some pollutants may cause more damage if they are heavily concentrated in one geographical area, rather than being more widely spread.

Chapter

12

Unit 1: Introductory concepts → Markets generally work well → Sometimes markets fail
→ This may justify government intervention → **Government failure sometimes occurs**

Government failure

Government failure

Government failure occurs when government intervention imposes a cost greater than the benefits brought about through the intervention. Thus the government intervention itself causes a **misallocation of resources** and a net loss of **economic welfare**.

It is difficult to prove that any particular policy is an example of government failure. However, we can use economic theory and empirical ('real world') evidence to suggest cases where it as at least possible that government failure has occurred.

Sources of government failure

The main sources of government failure are:

● **Inadequate information** about the extent of the market failure being tackled and the consequences of the policy.

● **Conflicting objectives** – this could be conflict between different economic objectives or conflict between political and economic objectives.

● The **administrative costs** of the policy.

Inadequate information

The extent of many market failures is difficult to identify, making it difficult to intervene appropriately. Consider the following examples:

● To what extent would education be under provided in the free market? What level of funding from the government would help bring about an optimal resource allocation?

● How much alcohol consumption is optimal? The answer is probably not zero, given that people do derive utility from consumption and that there are benefits in terms of social interaction.

● What is the optimal level of carbon dioxide emissions? Again, the answer is almost certainly not zero given that this would imply ceasing all activities which generate emissions.

It is clear from the above points that it is not possible to have information to give definitive answers to these questions. Governments also lack clear information about the effects of their policies, which sometimes cause **unintended consequences**. For example:

● Tightening environmental regulations for firms may simply lead them to locate elsewhere, where regulation is loose or does not exist at all. Taxing firms for polluting may have similar effects. The net effect may be more damage to the environment.

● Regulation to prohibit drug use means that users can only purchase drugs on the black market. This means they cannot have full knowledge of the nature of the drugs they buy. Impure drugs may lead to severe health problems or death. The high price of addictive drugs on the black market may also cause users to turn to crime in order to finance their habit, generating negative externalities.

● Raising taxes on demerit goods may cause consumers to buy them from countries where taxes are lower, thus the policy may not be effective in lowering consumption, but may lead to a reduction of government revenue.

● Government organisations, such as regulatory bodies and the NHS, are notorious for waste, using the resources given to them inefficiently because of the absence of the profit motive.

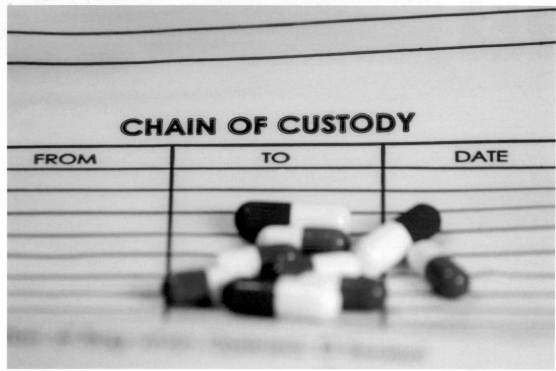

A ban on the sale and use of drugs would require policing.

Conflicting objectives

Governments have numerous economic objectives and these may sometimes come into conflict with each other. For example, government intervention to improve **equity** frequently distorts economic incentives and may cause **inefficiency**. The availability of benefits may reduce the incentive to work, for instance. This is one case of what is known as the **equity-efficiency trade-off**.

Political objectives and considerations may also interfere with economic policy making. For instance, the intervention buying price in minimum price or buffer stock schemes is often set too high due to pressure from producers. This serves to raise prices to consumers and leads to the production of excess supply which may have to be destroyed, wasting resources.

Governments may also be tempted to put into place policies which make them popular in the short term but may be economically damaging in the long term. At a macro level, expansionary monetary and fiscal policy in the run up to elections may cause problems in the future. This makes a case for independent policy making, for example central banks having the power to set interest rates. At a micro level, subsidising a failing industry is popular with those who depend on it for a livelihood but is not necessarily economically efficient.

The administrative costs of policy

The administrative costs of a policy can sometimes be substantial and may contribute to a situation where the policy as a whole carries costs in excess of the benefits. Examples of the administrative costs of policy include:

● The cost of enforcing regulations. A ban on the sale and use of drugs for example, requires policing and cases must be brought before the courts for those caught.

● The resources used in the process of policy making may themselves be substantial. For example, in setting a price cap for the water industry OFWAT must undertake substantial research, using significant labour resources.

● Wasted resources due to the lack of a profit motive in the public sector. Given the opportunity, the private sector may produce more health care than the public sector using the same resources, for example.

Chapter

13

Unit 1: This chapter links to all the following areas:
Markets generally work well → Sometimes markets fail → This may justify
government intervention → Government failure sometimes occurs

Wages and the national minimum wage

This chapter is targeted primarily at those following the Edexcel AS Level specification. At the time of writing, Edexcel is the only major exam board that identifies wage determination and government intervention in the labour market as a topic for AS Level study.

In a competitive labour market, wages are determined by the **market forces** associated with labour supply and demand. The **wage** is simply the **price** of labour.

Labour demand

Labour is a **derived demand**. Employers demand workers not for their own sake, but rather because of the output they produce and the contribution they make to the profits of the firm. Thus the demand for labour is derived from the demand for the products and services that labour helps generate. For example, if there was no demand for legal services, there would not be a demand for lawyers.

The demand for any type of labour is likely to increase when the revenue it generates for the firm increases. This could be due to a higher price for the product that the labour makes or it could be because **labour productivity** (output per worker) has increased.

Consider the example of demand for pilots. This will increase if demand for flights increases, thereby raising air fares ($D_1 \rightarrow D_2$):

Figure 13.1

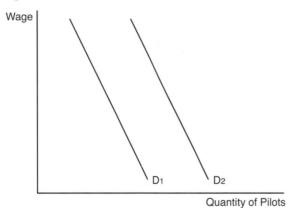

Labour supply

Potential workers must choose whether to supply their labour. If they do so, they sacrifice their leisure time and the wage they receive can be seen as compensation for doing so.

Influences on labour supply include:

- **Population migration.** Inwards migration tends to increase labour supply and outwards migration decreases it. The UK experienced a significant inwards migration of plumbers and construction workers when the European Union admitted new member states from Eastern Europe.

- **Birth rates.** Lower birth rates tend to reduce labour supply.

- **Skill requirements and training periods.** Occupations that require substantial qualifications and have lengthy training periods are likely to have restricted labour supply. This is the case with doctors, for instance.

- **Income tax.** This has the potential to reduce labour supply as it reduces the take-home wage for each hour worked, making leisure relatively more attractive.

● **Benefit payments.** These may also reduce labour supply as it becomes more affordable to make the choice not to work.

● **Trade unions** may attempt to restrict the labour supply to particular occupations in order to force the wage up for their members. In doing so, the union is attempting to act as a monopoly supplier of labour.

● **Government regulations**, such as the national minimum wage. Legally, there can be no supply of labour at wage rates below the national minimum wage.

Some of the points above can be applied to the example of airline pilots. The supply of pilots is likely to be limited because of the skill requirements and lengthy training period involved. Unions for pilots may also be powerful and therefore able to restrict the supply of labour significantly. Labour supply may be further limited by government regulations imposed for safety reasons, such as upper age limits for piloting aeroplanes and minimum requirements for the standard of eyesight and general health. Government taxation policy, particularly for high income earners, may affect the supply of pilots. A tax cut might increase supply.

The skill requirements and lengthy training for pilots may also mean that their labour supply is fairly inelastic: an increase in wage does not immediately result in large numbers of new trained pilots being available. The labour supply for pilots is illustrated in Figure 13.2.

Figure 13.2

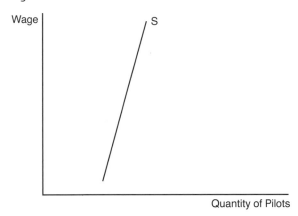

**Wage deter-
mination**

Figure 13.3

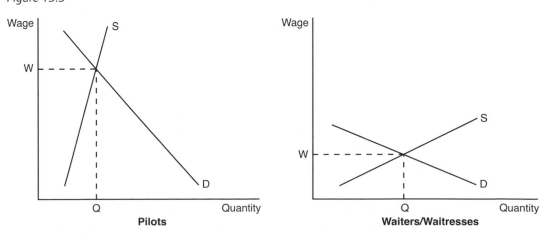

The wages for different occupations differ widely. While pilots are very well paid, for example, waiters and waitresses tend to receive relatively low pay. This can easily be explained using supply and demand analysis. As explained in the preceding sections, the supply of pilots tends to be limited, while the demand for pilots is boosted by the high levels of revenue they generate for their employers. Meanwhile, the low wages of waiting staff are explained largely by the fact that the job requires few formal qualifications and the fact that it offers flexible hours (thereby, attracting labour supply from those looking for part-time employment). Further, the tips received by waiting staff will tend to increase labour supply for any given wage. Figure 13.3 provides further analysis.

Market failure in the labour market

The fact that the wages paid to different workers differ so widely is regarded by many as a source of labour market failure, due to a lack of **equity**. It may be thought of as unfair that some workers can earn in a week ten times more than others can earn in a year.

Government intervention to cure this market failure takes a number of forms. One is a system of **progressive taxation** which takes a higher proportion of income from top income earners than from lower earners. Another is the payment of **benefits** to workers with low incomes. The national minimum wage is both an example of a **government regulation** and a **price control** as it sets a legally enforceable wage floor in the labour market.

The national minimum wage

The national minimum wage (NMW) means that labour cannot legally be supplied at a lower wage rate. On the assumption that the NMW is set above the equilibrium wage for low paid workers, economic theory predicts that this **wage floor** will cause a contraction of demand and an extension of labour supply, as shown in Figure 13.4. Thus it is possible that the NMW will generate unemployment in the form of an excess supply of labour ($Q_2 - Q_1$).

Figure 13.4

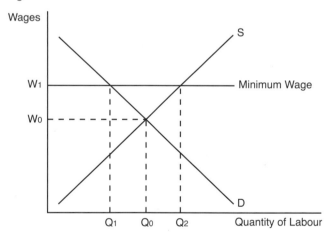

Economic arguments for and against raising the national minimum wage (NMW)	Arguments in favour of increasing the national minimum wage	Arguments against increasing the national minimum wage
	An increase in the NMW may help to alleviate poverty amongst those who benefit from the increase. This is desirable as it helps to tackle the market failure lack of equity.	An increase in the NMW has the potential to cost jobs by raising the costs of the firm. Unemployment may be created, as shown in Figure 13.4. The extent of this depends largely on the elasticity of labour demand.
	Male-female wage differentials will be reduced given that more females are beneficiaries of the NMW than males. Again this may improve fairness.	Any unemployment created may hit younger workers disproportionately, because their lack of experience makes them less valuable to firms.
	An increase in the NMW increases the reward for working, thereby improving incentives to work.	Many beneficiaries of the NMW are not the main wage earners in their household and are not poor. They may be people with well paid spouses or partners, and not need the support provided by a higher NMW.
	An improvement in the incentive to work may generate more tax revenue and result in fewer benefit payments.	Better paid workers may fight to restore pay differentials between themselves and beneficiaries of the NMW. This could be inflationary.
	Workers receive a boost to morale through higher wages. They may become more productive as the NMW increases.	An increase in the NMW may reduce the international price competitiveness of UK firms when compared to firms in countries with lower wages. This may cause a deterioration in the current account of the balance of payments.
	An increase in the NMW, by making workers more content, will reduce labour turnover for companies. This will lead to lower recruitment and training costs.	A disproportionate number of low paid workers are employed by the state. The NMW could have a negative effect on public sector finances (see Chapter 24).

As demonstrated in the table above, there are numerous arguments that can be advanced about whether the national minimum wage should be increased. Empirical ('real world') evidence has a significant role to play in the debate. The effects of previous increases in the NMW or increases in other countries with minimum wages could be examined.

It is important to be aware that the NMW is highly controversial. While for some it is a vital tool in reducing poverty and bringing about equity in the labour market, others would argue that the costs of the policy outweigh its benefits. Those who argue this would hold the national minimum wage to be a source of **government failure**.

Unit 2: Measuring the macroeconomy → How the macroeconomy works → Macroeconomic performance → Macroeconomic policy tools

Macroeconomic indicators

Macro-economic indicators

Macroeconomics deals with the performance of the economy as a whole. The four main indicators used to measure macroeconomic performance are:

● Economic growth (measured via national income)

● Unemployment

● Inflation

● The current account of the balance of payments.

Macro-economic objectives

Governments have objectives in relation to each of these four key variables, preferring **strong and sustainable economic growth, low unemployment, low and stable inflation and an acceptable balance of payments position** (this may imply avoiding large and persistent deficits).

Other government objectives may include achieving an **acceptable distribution of income**.

Measuring economic growth

Economic growth is measured as the change in national income over time.

The main measure of national income is **Gross Domestic Product** (**GDP**). This is defined as the value of output produced within the domestic boundaries of the UK over a period of time, usually a year. It includes the output of foreign firms that are located in the UK, such as Nissan in Sunderland. It does not include the output of UK firms that are located abroad.

An alternative measure of national income is **Gross National Product** (**GNP**), also known as **Gross National Income** (**GNI**). It measures the value of income from UK owned factors of production over a given period of time, usually a year. GNP is concerned with the income generated by UK owned factors of production regardless of whether they are located in the UK or overseas. It excludes the output of foreign firms located in the UK, but includes the output of UK firms located abroad.

GNI = GDP + Net property income from abroad (NPIA)

Net property income from abroad is the net balance of **interest**, **profits and dividends** (**IPD**) coming into the UK from UK assets owned overseas matched against the outflow of profits and other incomes from foreign owned assets located within the UK. For example, if a British-owned company operating in Germany sends some of its profits back to the UK this adds to UK GNI. Similarly, when a Japanese company located in the UK sends profits to Japan this will reduce UK GNI.

It is important to know that it is true by identity (definition) that national income, output and expenditure are equal to one another:

National Output = National Income = National Expenditure

This is most easily understood using the **circular flow of income**, as explained in Chapter 16.

Measuring unemploy-ment

The unemployed are those of a working age who are actively seeking work but do not have a job. Working age is defined as 16-65 for males, with the female retirement age in the process of being raised from 60 to 65. By 2046, the working age will be 16-68 for both males and females.

The unemployed are those of a working age who are actively seeking work but do not have a job.

Unemployment is a **stock** concept: it measures the number of people who are out of work at a given period of time. However, each month workers lose their jobs while others find new employment. Unemployment will fall if the **flow** of workers finding employment is greater than the number of workers losing their jobs.

The claimant count measure of unemployment simply counts the numbers claiming unemployment related benefit.

The **Labour Force Survey (LFS) method** is based on a monthly survey of 6000 households and uses the International Labour Organisation (ILO) definition of unemployment. It covers those who have looked for work in the past four weeks and are available to start work in the next two weeks.

Problems with the claimant count include:

● It is open to manipulation by politicians, as they can change the rules on who is entitled to claim benefits.

● It may understate unemployment because not everyone entitled to claim benefit does so.

● It may understate unemployment because some unemployed people are not entitled to benefit, for example if their spouse is in well paid employment.

● It may overstate unemployment because some people claim benefit fraudulently.

● Part-time workers who wish to work full time are not included in the statistics. These workers are classed as **underemployed**. This is a problem that is common to the claimant count and LFS (ILO) method.

Although the LFS (ILO) method gives an internationally recognised statistic, it is calculated using a survey of only 6000 households, so there is a possibility that it may not be truly representative.

Measuring inflation

Inflation is a persistent increase in the general level of prices over time.

The main measures of inflation are the Retail Price Index (RPI) and the government's preferred measure, the Consumer Price Index (CPI).

Retail Price Index (RPI)

● The RPI measures the **average** change in prices of a representative sample ('basket') of over 670 goods and services.

● Each month, a market research company collects over 130,000 separate price samples. These are then used to compile the inflation statistics which measure the change in prices over the preceeding 12 months.

● The index is **weighted** according to the proportion of income spent by the average household on categories of goods and services, such as food and housing. The weights are determined by the Expenditure and Food Survey that samples around 7000 households each year. Certain households are excluded from the survey. These include those households within the top 4% of incomes and pensioners. These groups are excluded to make the RPI more representative of the average household.

● The goods included in the index are changed over time to reflect changing consumer spending habits. In 2008, digital portable storage devices (camera memory cards, USB memory sticks and so on) were included for the first time.

● The weights are amended periodically to reflect changing spending patterns in the economy. The weight attached to leisure items tends to increase if the economy grows, because leisure spending is income elastic.

Other measures of inflation centred on the RPI include:

● The **RPIX**, which excludes mortgage interest payments.

● The **RPIY**, which excludes mortgage interest payments and indirect taxes.

Consumer Price Index (CPI)

The CPI is calculated using essentially the same price data as the RPI, but differs from it in some key respects. The differences include:

● the goods and services covered by the index. For instance, the CPI does not include Council Tax and a number of other housing costs faced by homeowners.

● the people whose expenditure is covered by the weights. The CPI covers a broader section of the population than the RPI.

● the mathematical formulae used to calculate the price changes in the two indices differ. This means that the CPI always shows a lower inflation rate than the RPI for any given set of price data.

Measuring the current account of the balance of payments

The current account primarily measures net trade in goods and services.

The current account is composed of four sections:

Trade in goods including items such as:	**Trade in services** including items such as:
● Manufactured goods ● Semi-finished goods and components ● Energy products ● Raw materials ● Consumer goods and capital goods	● Banking, insurance and consultancy ● Tourism ● Transport and shipping ● Education ● Cultural arts
Transfers. In the UK's case, we transfer significant money to the EU each year and also make foreign aid payments.	**International flows of wages, interest, profit and dividends.**

The trade in goods, or visible balance, records trade in tangible products.

The current account records the **flow of money** between countries, not the movement of goods and services. For example, the sale of a UK produced car to France (an export) would result in a flow of money into the UK, and this would, therefore, be represented as a **plus sign** in the current account. The fact that the car leaves the UK is irrelevant. Similarly if a UK consumer buys insurance from a German firm (an import), this would result in a flow of money out of the UK and would be represented as a **minus sign** in the current account.

The two main elements in the current account are:

● The **trade in goods section**, or visible balance, records trade in tangible products. Over the majority of the last 20 years the UK has had a **visible deficit**. This means that the **value of imported goods** exceeds the **value of exported goods**. For example, if the value of imported goods is £100bn and the value of exported goods is £70bn, then the trade in goods, or visible deficit, would be £30bn.

● The **trade in services section**, or invisible balance, measures trade in intangible services. The UK has traditionally experienced an **invisible surplus**. This means that the **value of exported services** exceeds the **value of imported services**. For example, if the value of exported services is £50bn and the value of imported services is £40bn, then the trade in services, or invisible surplus, would be £10bn.

At AS Level, students could explain these two sections and highlight that they combine to give the **current account balance**. During the majority of the last 20 years the UK has had a **current account deficit**. This occurs when the **value** of **imported goods and services** exceeds the **value of exported goods and services**.

Chapter

15

Unit 2: Measuring the macroeconomy → How the macroeconomy works →
Macroeconomic performance → Macroeconomic policy tools

Living standards and economic development

This chapter is primarily targeted at students following the **Edexcel** specification.

Income and wealth

It is important to understand that income and wealth are not the same thing. **Wealth** consists of a **stock of assets**. An economy's assets are the factors of production available to it.

Income is a **flow** derived from the stock of assets that make up wealth. These are factor payments earned by factors of production, which sum to give national income.

Wealthy countries tend to have high incomes because income is derived from the stock of assets that make up wealth, but income and wealth are not the same thing.

National income and living standards

It is common to use national income as an indicator of a country's living standards. **GDP per capita** (GDP divided by population) is the most frequently used variable for this purpose. However, it should be noted that GDP per capita figures are only an indication of **material living standards** and tell us nothing about the non-material aspects of quality of life. Even comparing material living standards is difficult.

GDP per capita figures may not give an accurate comparison even of material living standards

Difficulties in using GDP per capita figures to measure material living standards include:

● **The figures take no account of the distribution of income.** The income of a country with a high GDP per capita figure may be concentrated in the hands of small section of the population, with the rest of the population being poor. This tends to be the case in oil rich countries, for example. In the UK there are significant pockets of poverty, despite our high per capita GDP. The degree of inequality can be examined using the concepts of the **Lorenz curve and Gini coefficient** (see later in this chapter).

● **GDP figures understate national income because they do not include black market activity.** Such unrecorded activity would significantly boost the recorded national income if included.

● **GDP figures understate national income because they do not include the value of non-traded output.** We all produce valuable economic output that we do not trade. If households paid someone else to do all their washing, ironing, cooking, cleaning, decorating and other maintenance currently undertaken on a do-it-yourself basis, this would add hugely to national income. In developing countries, subsistence agriculture (families growing crops for consumption rather than trade) means that GDP figures significantly underestimate income.

● **Price changes can make it difficult to compare GDP per capita over time.** This means that GDP per capita figures should be adjusted for inflation to give real GDP per capita.

● **It is necessary to convert GDP per capita figures into a common currency in order to make international comparisons possible.** The American dollar is often used for this purpose.

● **The choice of the exchange rate for making the converting to a common currency crucially affects the outcome.** Converting the UK GDP per capita at £1 = $1.80 instead of £1 = $1.50 would give a 20% higher per capita income in dollars. The correct exchange rate to use is the **purchasing power parity** (**PPP**) exchange rate, which adjusts for price differentials between countries (PPP exchange rates give the same purchasing power for any given sum of money when it is converted into another currency). The GDP per capita of developing countries tends to be higher when using purchasing power parity rates for conversion than when using market exchange rates. This is because any given sum of money has greater purchasing power in developing countries due to the low price levels there.

● **International comparisons can be difficult due to differences in accounting procedures and accuracy of GDP statistics collected in different countries.**

Non-material aspects of standard of living, including environmental, social, education and health indicators

There is clearly more to having a good standard of living than how many goods and services a society is able to produce and consume. A more complete picture would take account to a variety of other factors. These might include:

● **Environmental indicators** such as air quality, water quality, greenhouse gas emissions, access to green space and areas of outstanding natural beauty, biodiversity (number of different species of plants and wildlife, for example) and so on. A moderate climate is generally thought to be an advantage.

● **Social indicators** such as crime rates, divorce rates and quality of human relationships (although this is very difficult to measure). 'Work-life balance' has become a particular issue in developed nations. This links to the length of the average working week and by implication to the amount of leisure time enjoyed.

● **Educational indicators** such as literacy and numeracy rates, percentage of the relevant age group enrolled in primary, secondary and higher education and so on. The rate of primary school enrolment is particularly important in developing countries.

● **Health indicators** such as life expectancy and infant mortality rates and indicators relating to particular illnesses such as heart disease (heart disease is a particular concern in richer, developed nations). The incidence of depression and stress-related illnesses also receives particular attention in developed nations.

● **Political freedoms** such as the right to vote, free speech and so on.

It is possible to argue that enjoying a high national income often comes at the expense of non-material aspects of quality of living. High levels of economic activity may contribute to environmental damage through negative externalities such as **resource depletion** (fewer resources available in the future, especially non-renewables such as fossil fuel) and **resource degradation** (polluted rivers are less useful, for example). High material living standards may be achieved through long working hours, contributing to stress related illnesses.

Measuring inequality: the Lorenz curve and the Gini coefficient

Figure 15.1

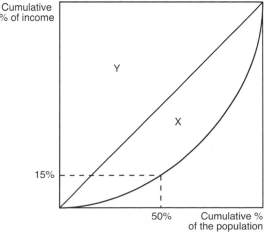

The degree of inequality in an economy can be examined by looking at the **Lorenz Curve**. In Figure 15.1, the cumulative percentage of income is plotted along the y-axis and the cumulative percentage of the population is plotted along the x-axis. A diagonal 45° line represents complete equality in income distribution because the poorest 10% of the population receive 10% of the income, while the richest 10% also only receive 10% of the income.

The further the curve bows away from 45°, the greater the level of inequality. In this diagram there is significant inequality as the poorest 50% of the population only earn 15% of total income. There is a numerical measure of inequality derived from the Lorenz Curve called the **Gini Coefficient**.

This is calculated by dividing area X by area Y in the diagram. Area X lies between the Lorenz Curve and the 45° line while Y is the total area above the 45° line. If the Gini coefficient is **zero** then there is complete **equality** and if it is one there is **total inequality** (one person enjoys all the income). It is easy to remember that the greater the Gini Coefficient the more the inequality.

The Human Development Index (HDI)

The **Human Development Index** (**HDI**) is an indicator of economic development published by the United Nations. It is an indicator composed of three variables:

● **Gross Domestic Product per capita**, measured in US dollars, using purchasing power parity exchange rates for conversions.

● **Life expectancy** in years.

● The **adult literacy** rate.

The HDI gives a better picture of a country's development and living standards than using GDP per capita alone. It is possible for countries to be ranked very differently in an 'HDI league table' compared to one for GDP. Oil rich nations, for example, tend to do well in GDP terms but relatively badly on HDI.

However, the HDI is far from being a complete measure of development. There are many factors discussed in the preceding sub-sections that it does not include. Countries could fare well in HDI terms, but still have poor living standards in many other respects. It would be possible, for instance, for a country with a high HDI figure to have very low environmental standards and not offer political freedoms to its citizens.

Other measures of development

For developing countries, economists may pay particular attention to indicators that seem less relevant in richer, developed economies. Such indicators include:

● The percentage of adult male labour in agriculture. As an economy develops, workers tend to move out of the primary sector of the economy and into the secondary and tertiary sectors.

● Primary and secondary school enrolment figures have implications for literacy, numeracy and other valuable skills and make a significant difference to the future productive capacity of the economy.

● Access to clean water is particularly important in societies where not all citizens have their basic economic needs met and absolute poverty is a concern.

● Energy consumption per capita, which tends to increase as countries become more economically developed.

● Access to mobile phones per thousand of the population. Communication links are valuable both for social reasons and for the organisation of economic activity.

Chapter 16

Unit 2: Measuring the macroeconomy → **How the macroeconomy works** → Macroeconomic performance → Macroeconomic policy tools

The circular flow of income and aggregate demand (AD)

The circular flow of income

The circular flow model looks at the interaction between members of households and firms.

Members of households supply **factors of production to firms**, receiving income (**factor payments**) in return. The various factor payments are shown below:

Factor	Payment
Land	Rent
Labour	Wages and salaries
Capital	Interest
Enterprise	Profit

The firms combine the factors of production into **output**, which households spend their money on. This is known as **expenditure**. Firms then return this money to households in the next round of factor payments (**income**), setting up a circular flow.

The circular flow helps us to understand the national income identity:

National output = National income = National expenditure

The income received by households funds the expenditure on the output produced by firms. Income, output and expenditure are thus the same flow measured at three different points.

Note also that:

● Households do not spend all of their income. They save some at banks and other financial institutions. This money can be lent out to firms for investment projects.

● The government sector is also important through their taxation and spending decisions.

● There is spending on imported goods and services and injections of demand into the economy from the sale of exports.

The circular flow is shown in Figure 16.1.

Figure 16.1

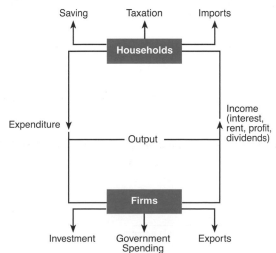

Injections and withdrawals	The circular flow of income highlights the main injections and withdrawals in an economy.

Injections
Exports (X)
Investment (I)
Government spending (G)

Withdrawals
Imports (M)
Savings (S)
Taxation (T)

Injections will add money to the circular flow of income while withdrawals will remove money from it. If **injections are greater than withdrawals**, expenditure on goods and services will exceed the planned level of production. Firms will, therefore, expand output and **national income will rise**. Conversely if **withdrawals are greater than injections**, production will exceed the current level of expenditure. Firms will, therefore, reduce their output and **national income will fall**.

The aggregate demand curve

Aggregate Demand is the **total spending on goods and services** in an economy over a given period of time. It is calculated using the following formula:

**AD = Consumer expenditure (C) + Investment (I)
+ Government expenditure (G) + (Exports (X) – Imports (M))**

C   **Consumer spending** – is spending on goods and services that are used for the **direct satisfaction** of individual or collective needs. It is also known as **household final consumption expenditure**. This includes personal expenditure on durable and non-durable goods, as well as on services.

I   **Gross Domestic Fixed Capital Formation** – is investment spending on assets that are used repeatedly or continuously over a number of years to produce goods. For example, spending by companies on **capital goods** such as machinery and vehicles. Investment also includes spending on **working capital** such as **stocks** of finished goods and work in progress.

G   **General Government Final Consumption** – is current spending on publicly provided goods and services. It also includes spending on public sector employment.

X   **Exports of goods and services** – this is UK produced output that is sold abroad. Exports are an **injection** into the circular flow of income.

M   **Imports of goods and services** – this is foreign produced output that is purchased by UK consumers and firms. Imports are a **withdrawal** from the circular flow of income.

Figure 16.2

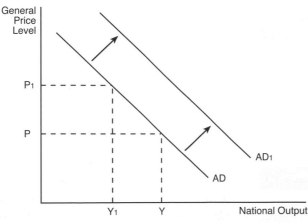

Figure 16.2 illustrates an **aggregate demand curve**. It is very much like an ordinary demand curve, but the axes on the diagram are different. National output is placed on the x-axis and the general price level is represented on the y-axis.

The AD curve is **downward sloping**. A rise in the price level from P to P₁ will lead to a fall in the total demand for goods and services from Y to Y₁. This is because:

● at higher price levels the total demand for goods and services will be lower.

● as the price level becomes higher, British goods become **less competitive**. Higher imports and lower exports will reduce AD.

A number of factors will cause the AD curve to shift:

● The **aggregate demand curve** will shift to the **right** from AD to AD₁ when there is a rise in **consumption**, or any of the three injections into the circular flow of income, namely **investment**, **government spending or exports**.

● A **rise in imports** will shift the **aggregate demand curve to the left**. This is because imports are a withdrawal from the circular flow of income and will reduce the total demand for UK goods and services.

For example:

Event	AD shift	Explanation
Income tax cut	Right	The income tax cut will increase disposable income, boosting consumption.
Interest rate rise	Left	A higher interest rate raises the opportunity cost of spending (saving more attractive, borrowing expensive). Consumption and investment both fall.
An increase in the budget deficit	Right	Government spending has risen relative to taxation. The government provides a bigger net injection to the circular flow.
A stronger pound	Left	The stronger pound makes imports cheaper and exports more expensive. Net exports (X-M) fall.
An increase in the general price level	AD does **not** shift but does contract	Changes in the general price level cause a movement along the AD curve.

The factors that influence the components of aggregate demand will be analysed more fully in later chapters.

Remember that a change in the general price level will not itself shift the AD curve. The general price level is on the y-axis and thus varies along the length of the curve. A change in the general price level would create an extension or a contraction of AD rather than a shift of the curve.

The multiplier effect

An initial injection into the circular flow of income will cause a greater change in aggregate demand and national income.

The multiplier is defined as the ratio of the change in national income to the change in expenditure that brought it about.

Many examples can be used to illustrate the multiplier. Most importantly you must be able to describe in simple terms the **multiplier process**. Consider the effects of an increase in investment by a firm on new machines of £100m. This will raise national income by £100m since the **expenditure of one group is the income of another**. The process will not stop here though. The initial expenditure will **generate incomes** that will be used to finance spending in future time periods. This adds to the effects on total GDP.

The size of the multiplier effect is determined by the rate of leakages or withdrawals from the economy.

At each stage of the process, as income is earned through additional spending, some will leak out of the circular flow of income in the form of **savings** (incomes not spent), **taxation** (taken out by the Government sector) and **imports** (the demand for foreign produced goods and services). Thus the **size of the multiplier effect** is determined by the **rate of leakages or withdrawals from the economy**. The multiplier in a modern economy tends to be small. This is largely because modern economies are open to trade and a considerable proportion of spending is on imports, which serve to reduce the value of the multiplier as they are a leakage from the circular flow.

Chapter

17

Unit 2: Measuring the macroeconomy → **How the macroeconomy works** →
Macroeconomic performance → Macroeconomic policy tools

Aggregate supply (AS) and macro equilibrium

Aggregate supply curve (AS)

Like ordinary supply curves in microeconomics, the macroeconomic aggregate supply (AS) curve slopes upwards from left to right. This is because, ceteris paribus, higher prices increase the profitability of supplying output.

Figure 17.1

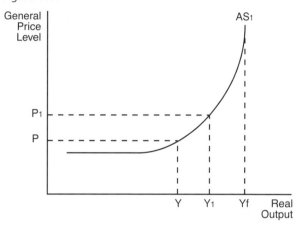

The AS curve is **elastic** (flat) at relatively low levels of output, implying that there are substantial amounts of **spare capacity** in the economy. Output can expand quickly in the short run without a substantial rise in the price level.

As the economy moves closer to the **full employment** of the factors of production the AS curve becomes more **inelastic** (steep). Firms start to experience **supply bottlenecks** and there are shortages of raw materials and labour. This means that firms' costs of production start to rise and, in order to maintain their profit margins, they cannot raise production without increasing their prices.

Eventually when all the factors of production are fully employed (at Yf in Figure 17.1) it is impossible for firms to produce any extra output and the AS curve will become perfectly inelastic. At this point, the economy is operating on its **production possibility frontier**. Yf corresponds to the economy's productive potential (capacity), which is determined by the **quantity and quality of factors of production** available.

Shifts of the AS curve

The aggregate supply curve will shift to the **right** when **costs of production fall**. Thus the curve would shift in response to changes to payments to any factors of production or in response to changes to their productivity.

For example, higher wage rates or oil prices would reduce aggregate supply. So too might an increase in strike action, as this would reduce labour productivity. The opposite of these factors would increase AS, as shown in Figure 17.2.

If a fall in the cost of production has resulted from an increase in the quantity or quality of factors of production, rather than just a fall in their price, then the potential capacity of the economy when operating at full employment has increased, and the shift could be drawn as in Figure 17.3.

Figure 17.2

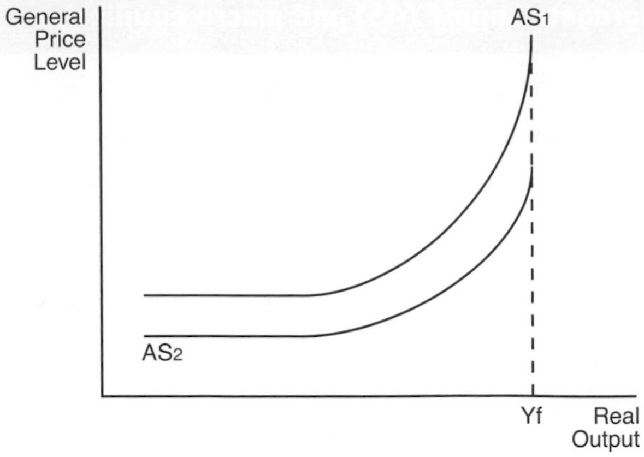

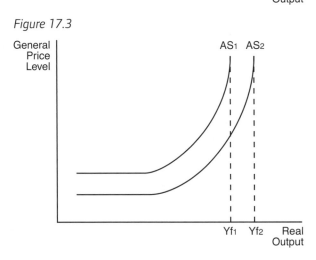

Figure 17.3

Macro-economic equilibrium

Macroeconomic equilibrium is achieved when aggregate supply is equal to aggregate demand. The equilibrium is disturbed if one of the curves shifts.

Shifts of the AD curve tend to produce trade-offs with regard to the four main economic indicators. For example, an increase of AD is likely to increase real output and reduce unemployment because of a higher derived demand for labour. However, it will create inflationary pressure, especially if there is only a small output gap. The current account of the balance of payments may deteriorate as higher prices reduce competitiveness and higher demand leads to the 'sucking in' of imports.

On the other hand, shifts of AS tend to improve or worsen all four main economic indicators simultaneously. An increase in the economy's capacity, for instance, allows higher growth (generating employment) and relieves inflationary pressure. Improved competitiveness and available capacity to serve the export market are likely to improve the current account of the balance of payments.

Shifts of AD produce trade-offs

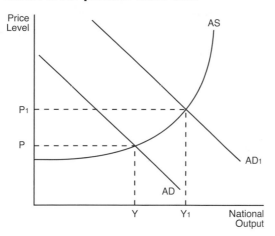

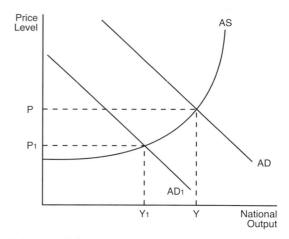

When AD increases:

• Increased output and reduced unemployment.

But

• Inflationary pressure and deterioration of the current account of the balance of payments.

When AD falls:

• Reduced inflationary pressure and improved current account of balance of payments.

But

• Lower output and higher unemployment.

Shifts of AS may move all four main indicators in the same direction

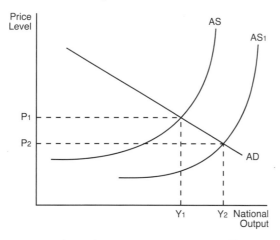

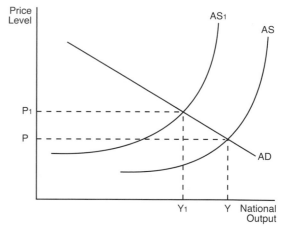

• Potential simultaneous improvement in all four main macroeconomic indicators.

• Potential simultaneous deterioration in all four main macroeconomic indicators.

An alternative version of AS

Later chapters of this book draw the AS curve as it was drawn in Digram 17.1 through to 17.3. However, there is an alternative version that makes a distinction between short run aggregate supply (SRAS) and long run aggregate supply (LRAS).

The AQA specification makes a short and long run distinction when studying aggregate supply, so read this section carefully if you are studying for the AQA exam. However, the same factors still shift aggregate supply as before, and rightwards shifts of aggregate supply still have the potential to simultaneously improve all four main economic indicators.

Short run aggregate supply (SRAS)

For this purpose, the **short run** is defined as the period of time in which the price of factors of production is fixed. Thus short run aggregate supply (SRAS) curves are drawn for a given cost of production. SRAS extends as the general price level increases, because a rise in the price level increases the profit margin on each unit supplied at the given cost of production.

Any change in production costs will shift the SRAS curve. Thus the curve would shift in response to changes to payments to any factors of production or in response to changes to their productivity.

Any factor reducing production costs will shift the SRAS curve to the right as shown in Figure 17.4.

Remember that a change in the general price level itself will not shift the curve.

Figure 17.4

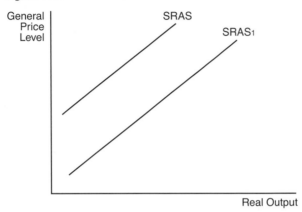

Long run aggregate supply (LRAS)

In the long run, the prices of all factors of production can change. If it is assumed that they adjust to bring about equilibrium in the markets for the factors of production, then in the long run resources will be fully employed and the economy will operate at full productive potential (capacity).

The productive potential of the economy is determined by the factors of production available to it. This means that the quantity and quality (productivity) of the economy's land, labour, capital and enterprise determines the position of the long run aggregate supply curve.

Accordingly, the LRAS curve would shift to the right (as shown in Figure 17.5) through investment in physical or human capital (the skills of the labour force). Increases in the population of working age or the discovery of new natural resources would have the same effect. Government policy can significantly affect the capacity of the economy. Lower corporate taxes or lighter regulation of businesses could encourage entrepreneurship, for example.

Figure 17.5

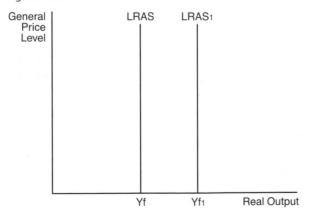

Anything that shifts the long run curve will also shift the short run curve. This is because an increase in capacity will also put downward pressure on the costs of production.

In the long run, the prices of all factors of production can change.

No long run trade-offs

The short and long run version of AS makes the point that there may be no trade-off between economic objectives in the long run.

Even if an increase in AD stimulated output and employment in the short term, its long run effect is purely inflationary and it may also lead to a deterioration of the current account of the balance of payments. Shifts of the LRAS are likely to lead to simultaneous improvement or deterioration in all four main indicators.

No long run trade-offs between economic objectives

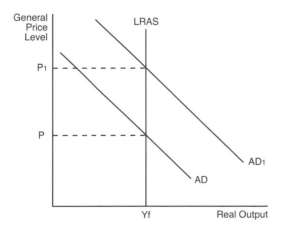

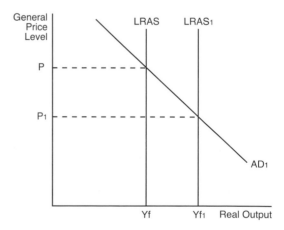

An increase in AD **fails** to increase output and reduce unemployment in the **long run**, **but** is inflationary and is likely to lead to a deterioration of the current account of the balance of payments.

An increase in LRAS is likely to improve all four main economic indicators simultaneously.

Chapter

18

Unit 2: Measuring the macroeconomy → **How the macroeconomy works** →
Macroeconomic performance → Macroeconomic policy tools

Consumption, saving and investment

Consumer spending

Consumer spending is also known as **household final consumption expenditure**. It includes **personal expenditure** on **durable and non-durable goods** as well as on **services**. Excluded are all business expenditure and expenses, interest payments and spending on dwellings.

Consumers purchase goods and services for the **direct satisfaction** of individual or collective needs, and expenditure on goods and services in the UK accounts for over **60% of GDP**. A change in consumer expenditure will, therefore, have a much greater impact on GDP than a similar variation in another component of aggregate demand.

Factors affecting consumption

1. Real disposable income

Consumption is likely to increase when real disposable income increases. Real income is money income adjusted for inflation, while disposable income means income after direct taxes and benefits.

Opinions differ as to the strength of the relationship between real disposable income and consumption. Keynes argued that the relationship was strong, but this was questioned by Milton Friedman. He suggested that increases in real income only influence consumption if they are believed to be permanent (the permanent-income hypothesis).

Suppose a government cuts taxes prior to a general election. This increases real disposable income but, according to Friedman, may not influence consumption. If consumers perceive this to be only a temporary reduction in their tax burden, purely to boost the government's popularity, then consumption will remain unchanged.

2. Interest rates

Most students can identify that a **rise in interest rates** will **reduce consumer expenditure**, but few can accurately explain precisely how this occurs. If the Bank of England announces a rise in interest rates there is likely to be:

- a **rise in saving**. This is because the **opportunity cost of spending has increased**. If consumers carry on spending they will forego more interest. As a result, saving will probably increase as individuals postpone current consumption in favour of spending in future time periods.

- a **fall in demand** for **consumer durables purchased on credit**. This is because **loan repayments**, on items such as TVs, fridges, cars and holidays, **will increase**.

- a fall in '**discretionary incomes**'. A rise in interest rates will increase **mortgage and other loan repayments**. Effectively, this means that consumers are left with less money in their pockets at the end of each month and consumer expenditure will fall.

All these factors should combine to **reduce the demand for assets** such as housing and shares. If the value of assets falls, consumers' wealth will diminish and, as a result, they may cut back on their spending.

3. Unemployment

A rise in the level of unemployment, or the increased threat of being made jobless, may encourage workers to hold higher **precautionary savings**, which will reduce current consumption. Conversely, a fall in unemployment boosts **consumer confidence** and increases spending.

These effects are also reinforced by the fact that changes in **unemployment** influence the **wages and salaries** earned by those in employment. When the demand for labour increases and unemployment falls, the growth of wages and earnings accelerates. This will boost the spending power of people in work and increase consumer expenditure. Rising unemployment in a recession causes a slowdown in income growth and encourages consumers to rein in their spending plans.

4. Tax burden

In theory, a **rise in direct taxes**, such as income tax and national insurance contributions, will reduce **real disposable income** and the level of consumption. A **rise in indirect taxes**, such as VAT, will directly **increase the prices** of goods and services. Consumers are, therefore, likely to cut back expenditure on those products that are affected by the tax, which reduces consumer expenditure.

A tax change may not always have the effect that an economist expects. A **direct tax cut** may not increase consumer expenditure if it is all saved. This may occur if a consumer is uncertain about the future or believes that a tax cut is transitory. Remember, if a tax cut is perceived to be temporary then it may not increase **permanent income** or consumption.

5. Population

The **age structure** of the population has an impact on household consumption. Many economists believe that consumer spending in future years may be limited by the rising number of 30-50 year olds and pensioners in the population. This can be explained by the **life cycle hypothesis**.

This hypothesis is based on the idea that the level of spending relative to income depends on where the consumer is in their **life cycle**. It suggests that consumers attempt to even out consumption over their lifetime and, as a result, will borrow and save at different ages.

● In the 18-30 age range, consumers will spend more than their current income. They undertake a large number of credit financed purchases; especially relating to housing.

● In middle age, consumers spend less than their current income. They repay their mortgage and other loans and increase **savings** for retirement. This traditional view is becoming less typical in modern society as inheritance and changing family structures, in particular divorce, increasingly influence spending behaviour. Both these factors may stimulate consumption in middle age.

● When consumers reach pensionable age they spend more than their current income. This is because their incomes fall quite sharply and they use up savings made in earlier years.

6. Wealth effects

The **wealth effects** of rising real asset values on consumer expenditure are difficult to quantify, but nevertheless important. When the value of **housing** and other assets (**shares**) is rising faster than income, individuals see a rise in their **net worth** (the difference between the value of their assets and liabilities). This increases consumer confidence and causes consumer expenditure to rise.

Rising house prices may also give rise to a phenomenon known as **mortgage equity withdrawal**. As house prices rise, consumers are able to obtain loans secured on the rising values of their properties. These loans can be used to purchase a wide range of goods and services and will boost consumer expenditure.

However, if asset prices fall, consumers can be left with a **net worth problem**. That is, they have liabilities or debts that exceed the value of their assets. To eliminate this problem consumers have to repay debts by saving. Higher saving means that consumer spending will have to fall.

7. Consumer confidence

Consumer confidence is strongly correlated with expenditure. When confidence is falling it is usually a reliable indicator of a fall in the growth of spending. If consumers become more pessimistic they are less likely to commit themselves to a major 'big-ticket' purchase.

Saving

Income is either consumed or saved. **Saving** is defined as the act of foregoing consumption. It is measured by the **personal sector savings ratio**. The formula is **saving divided by disposable income**.

Why do individuals save?
- for retirement
- for big ticket items
- for precautionary motives
- for capital gains
- for future generations

Those factors that promote high levels of consumption lead to low levels of saving.

Savings are important economically:

Private saving takes pressure off the taxpayer, for example to provide for people in their old age.

Savings are channelled by financial institutions to borrowers, many of whom wish to borrow to invest. Higher savings result in more funds available for investment.

Investment spending

Investment is defined as spending on assets which are used repeatedly or continuously over a number of years to produce goods and services. Increased investment in capital goods by firms and the government will allow greater production in future time periods.

Fixed Investment – is spending on new machinery, plant, buildings, vehicles, etc. that will be used continuously or repeatedly in a production process. This would include machinery in a factory, computers in an office and aeroplanes belonging to an airline.

Working Capital – is spending on stocks which are held by their producers before they are sold, stocks of raw materials and work in progress. The accumulation of stocks by firms, whether voluntary or involuntary, is counted as investment.

Net investment – is gross investment with capital depreciation subtracted. Capital depreciation relates to the reduction in the value of an asset due to wear and tear. Net investment must be positive for there to be an increase in the capital stock.

Factors affecting investment spending

1. Changes in aggregate demand
The **accelerator model** stresses that **investment in the economy is demand induced**. When firms have insufficient capacity, they must invest when demand increases, or they will not be able to satisfy the orders they receive. An increase in demand may therefore lead to a significant acceleration in the rate of investment, especially if spare capacity is limited and the economy's output gap (Chapter 19) is small.

2. Interest rates
Most students know that higher interest rates should have a negative impact on investment. Few, however, can explain accurately why this happens. The reasons are outlined below:

- Many firms raise finance for investment by borrowing from financial institutions. A rise in interest rates will increase the cost of financing such schemes. This means there will be a rise in the cost of investment relative to the yield and, as a result, some investment projects become unprofitable. A firm will only invest if the yield of a project exceeds the cost.

- A rise in the rate of interest increases the **opportunity cost** of using internal funds to finance investment projects. Some marginal investment projects may not take place as firms decide that they can attain a better rate of return by depositing their retained profits in a bank.

- Higher interest rates **reduce** the level of **aggregate demand**. This reduces investment via the **accelerator process**. Higher interest rates are also likely to **reduce business confidence and corporate profitability**. This applies further downward pressure on investment.

3. Profitability

A rise in the level of corporate profitability should have a positive impact on investment levels. A rise in profitability is usually a signal that the **rate of return** on investment projects will increase and hence more investment projects will become profitable. An increase in profits also allows the firm to invest using internal funds, which are usually cheaper than other forms of corporate finance.

4. Business confidence

This has a strong positive impact on investment levels. Levels of confidence are a function of the factors that we have previously discussed.

5. Corporate taxation

A **fall in corporation tax** will **increase the post-tax rate of return** of a new investment with the result that more investment projects become viable. Tax allowances also influence the extent to which firms can afford to write off depreciating machinery and replace equipment on a regular basis.

The economic effects of investment

Why do firms invest?

A positive level of net investment implies a rise in the firm's **capital stock** and a long run expansion. The reasons for undertaking an investment project are varied:

● To take advantage of **higher expected profits** from expanding output.

● To generate a **rise in productive capacity** to meet increased demand.

● To **improve efficiency** via technological progress.

● To **exploit economies of scale** (see Chapter 5).

● As part of a **long run process of capital/labour substitution**; perhaps in response to changes in the relative prices of the factors of production. Higher wage costs relative to capital costs could encourage this strategy.

● As a **barrier to entry** – some investment projects give firms significant cost advantages. This may deter potential competitors from entering a market (see Chapter 6 and the section on monopoly).

Changes in investment will have **short-term effects on the demand side** of the economy and more important **long-term effects on the supply side** of the economy.

Demand side effects

Figure 18.1

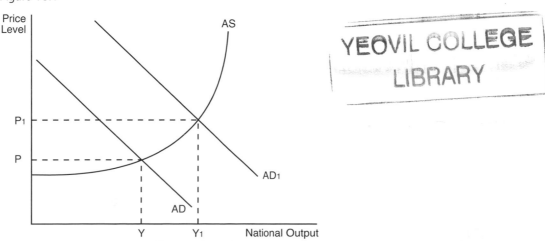

The short-term effects of a rise in investment are examined in Figure 18.1. Investment is a component of aggregate demand and a rise in this variable will shift the aggregate demand curve to the right from AD to AD_1. This will result in a rise in national output from Y to Y_1, and cause **economic growth** (Chapter 19).

The rise in national output will be greater than the change in investment because of the operation of the **multiplier**. There will also be some **demand pull inflation** (see Chapter 21) as the price level has increased from P to P₁.

Supply side effects

In the long run, a rise in net investment will increase the **productive capacity** of the economy and, if the new capital embodies new technology, it will also reduce the **costs of production**. A rise in capacity and/or a fall in costs will shift the AS curve to the right. This is illustrated in Figure 18.2. A rise in aggregate supply will cause a rise in national output from Y to Y₁ and a fall in the price level from P to P₁. This will help the economy to achieve growth without inflation.

Figure 18.2

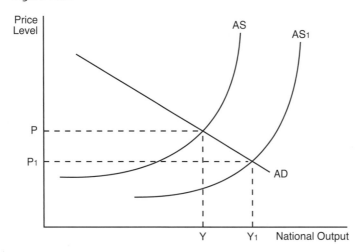

There is a strong positive correlation between investment levels and economic growth. Countries that invest a high proportion of their GDP tend to experience a higher rate of growth. Higher investment should also improve a nation's **international competitiveness**. This will help a country to expand exports of goods and services and compete more effectively against imports from other economies.

New capital machinery is likely to embody new technology. This allows firms who invest heavily to produce goods and provide services of higher quality. Spending which adds to the **stock of capital** can also create new employment in the **capital goods industries**. However, there may be a negative effect on total employment if the main driving force behind investment is to introduce **labour-saving** technology through **capital-labour substitution**.

Chapter

19

Unit 2: Measuring the macroeconomy → How the macroeconomy works →
Macroeconomic performance → Macroeconomic policy tools

Economic growth

Economic growth

Economic growth is measured as **the increase in real GDP** over a given period of time, usually a year. This figure is expressed as a percentage.

In the long run, the rate of economic growth is determined by the rate at which the economy's capacity (productive potential) increases.

Current (actual or short run) and trend (potential or long run) growth

- **Current growth** is usually caused by an increase in aggregate demand. This draws on the economy's spare capacity, closing the output gap, and bringing unemployed resources into use. Another way of looking at this is that it takes the economy closer to its production possibility frontier. Such growth is not sustainable and will be brought to an end once the economy has no more spare capacity. Further increases in aggregate demand would be purely inflationary once this point is reached.

- **Trend growth** (otherwise known as long run growth or the underlying rate of growth) can be defined in the following ways. (i) It is the long run average growth rate of an economy. (ii) It is the growth rate that the economy can sustain without generating inflationary pressure.

- The trend growth rate of an economy would be calculated using data over a substantial period of time, certainly at least one complete business cycle.

- An economy's trend growth rate is determined by the rate at which its capacity grows. A trend growth rate of 2.5%, for example, suggests that on average the capacity of the economy grows at 2.5% a year. Remember that an economy's capacity is a function of the quantity and quality (productivity) of the factors of production (land, labour, capital and enterprise) available.

- The fact that trend growth reflects capacity increases explains why trend growth is sustainable. Capacity increases mean that higher aggregate demand can be accommodated without inflationary pressure.

The economic cycle (the business or trade cycle)

The economy experiences regular cycles, which can be tracked using annual and quarterly movements in real output (GDP). The turning points in the cycle are known as peaks and troughs. Other key terms to be aware of are:

- **Recession.** This refers to falling output and is usually defined as at least two successive quarters of negative growth. (see A-B in Figure 19.1)

- **Recovery.** This is the period between the trough of the business cycle and the next peak. This period is also sometimes known as a boom, but the term 'boom' may be better used to describe a period of very rapid, above-trend growth (see point B onwards in Figure 19.1).

The business cycle shows us how GDP changes over time and therefore shows current growth, which largely reflects changes in aggregate demand. We should also be aware of the supply side, however. Recessions can be caused by supply side factors such as higher oil prices as well as by restricted aggregate demand.

The best fit line drawn through the business cycle shows the trend growth rate of the economy.

Figure 19.1

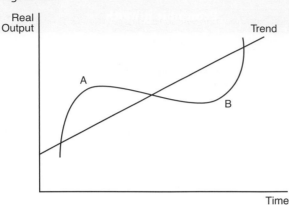

The output gap and the economic cycle

● The **output gap** is the difference between actual and potential real GDP.

● If the economy grows faster than trend for any significant period of time, this suggests aggregate demand is growing faster than capacity. This is likely to reduce unemployment, but may be inflationary as the output gap closes. There may even be a positive output gap, with the economy temporarily operating beyond full capacity (for example, through overtime work).

● Below trend growth suggests that demand is growing more slowly than capacity. The output gap grows and so too does unemployment, but inflationary pressure is reduced.

● If the economy grows at trend, no inflationary pressure is generated and economic stability is enhanced. Once again, trend growth is seen as the sustainable growth rate for the economy.

Figure 19.2

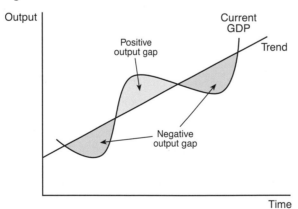

What determines the trend growth rate of the economy?

Given that trend growth is determined by the rate at which economic capacity increases, we need to look at the influences on the quantity and quality of factors of production to find out what determines trend growth.

Economies with high trend growth rates tend to:

● Invest a substantial proportion of their GDP, thus boosting the quantity and quality of their capital stock.

● Devote resources to research and development in order to achieve technological advances (although it is also possible to receive external benefits as a third party gaining from technological advances made by other countries).

● Have high quality education and training systems, raising the productivity of workers.

● Have 'flexible labour markets' with workers willing to adapt to new working practices, thereby enhancing their productivity.

● Benefit from a strong entrepreneurial culture, perhaps supported by a policy framework of low corporate taxes and only light regulation by the government.

● Possess a strong institutional structure. This might imply adequate protection of property rights, including patents for 'intellectual property' such as new ideas. There should also be a strong financial system to provide the finance that firms need in order to invest and innovate.

Advantages and disadvantages of economic growth

Advantages of Economic Growth

1. Higher economic growth should lead to an increase in **living standards** as measured by real GDP per capita. The problems with this measure of living standards are discussed in Chapter 15.

2. The effects of growth are **cumulative**. If a country grows at 3% per annum, the economy will double in size every 24 years. Growth helps make future investment more affordable.

3. Economic growth should reduce **unemployment**. When output in the economy increases there should be an increase in the demand for labour. This is because labour is a **derived demand**, that is the demand for labour is dependent on the final demand for goods and services. Firms do not demand labour for its own sake.

4. Economic growth will have a positive effect on **government finances**. Economic growth will **increase tax revenues** because as output, employment and incomes rise so will the tax take. Growth will reduce unemployment and, as a result, **expenditure on transfer payments** will fall. These two effects will combine to reduce the budget deficit (see Chapter 24). Alternatively the government could increase spending on areas such as education and health without having to put up taxes and reduce current consumption levels.

5. Rising demand and output encourages further **investment** in new capital machinery via the **accelerator process**. This will boost the productive capacity of the economy in the long run.

Disadvantages of Economic Growth

1. If current growth exceeds trend growth there is the danger of **inflation**. The rise in prices may reduce the **international competitiveness** of the economy.

2. Economic growth will create **negative externalities**, such as increased pollution and congestion, which will damage social welfare. Those affected could experience a fall in living standards.

3. The benefits of **economic growth may not be evenly distributed**. A rise in national output may also be associated with growing inequality in society. Just because there is economic growth, it does not mean that the number of people living **below the poverty line**, i.e. in absolute poverty, will diminish.

4. Faster economic growth might lead to an **over exploitation of scarce finite economic resources** that will limit growth prospects in the future.

Chapter

20

Unit 2: Measuring the macroeconomy → How the macroeconomy works →
Macroeconomic performance → Macroeconomic policy tools

Unemployment

Definition of unemployment

Unemployment consists of those of a working age who are actively seeking employment but do not have a job.

Chapter 14 gives details on how unemployment is measured.

Causes of unemployment and policy to reduce it

Unemployment has a number of different causes. It can result from a lack of demand (demand deficient unemployment) or various problems on the supply side of the economy (real-wage unemployment, frictional unemployment and structural unemployment).

The policies appropriate to tackling unemployment depend crucially on what has caused the unemployment in the first place.

Demand deficient unemployment

Demand deficient unemployment is associated with an **economic recession**. Labour is a **derived demand** – it is not demanded for its own sake, but because of the output that it produces. A fall in the level of output will cause a drop in the demand for labour at each wage level. As aggregate demand drops, firms will lay-off workers to reduce their costs and protect profits.

Figure 20.1

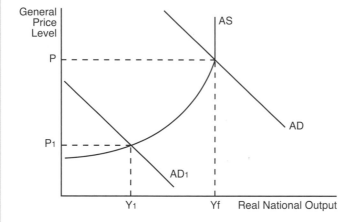

In Figure 20.1, the equilibrium level of national output (Y_1) lies below the full employment level of national output (Y_f). This means that there is insufficient aggregate demand for all workers to obtain employment. The current level of demand (AD_1) lies below the level required for full employment (AD).

Although demand deficient unemployment is usually associated with economic recessions it can also exist in the long run when the economy has an **output gap**. This occurs when actual output lies below potential output.

Policies for demand deficient unemployment

The usual government response is to raise aggregate demand. This can be achieved by utilising a variety of policy instruments.

● **Increase Government Expenditure** – this will boost aggregate demand because it is one of its components. The change in national output will be greater than the change in government expenditure because of the operation of the **multiplier**. The larger the value of the multiplier the greater the effect on national output. If the government raises expenditure on infrastructure, or training, it will also boost the productive potential of the economy and shift the AS curve to the right.

● **Reduce Taxation** – lower income taxes will increases consumers' real disposable incomes and boost consumer expenditure.

● **Lower interest rates** – will encourage borrowing, reduce saving and increase consumers' real discretionary incomes. This should boost consumer expenditure and the level of aggregate demand. A drop in interest rates may also encourage firms to invest, as the cost of investment will fall.

● **Depreciate the pound** – this should lead to a rise in export orders for UK firms and to a fall in imports. This is because a fall in the value of the currency will reduce the price of exports and increase the cost of imports.

Remember the effects of monetary and fiscal policy are not instantaneous. It will take some time for the full effect of these policies to impact on output and employment.

Real wage unemployment

Real wage unemployment is a form of **disequilibrium unemployment** that occurs when **real wages** are forced above **the market clearing level**. Traditionally, **trade unions** and **minimum wage legislation** have been seen as the main cause of this type of unemployment.

Suppose that having initially been in equilibrium where the demand for labour was equal to the supply of labour, a minimum wage W1 is set above the market clearing wage W. The effects of such an action are illustrated in Figure 20.2

Figure 20.2

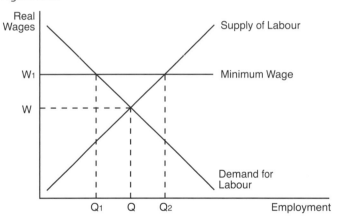

At the new minimum wage W1, the **demand for labour** has contracted from Q to Q1 while the supply of labour has expanded from Q to Q2. Firms will tend to employ fewer workers when the **marginal cost** of employing them increases. At the same time, more workers will be willing to take jobs at higher wage rates.

At real wage W1, there is an **excess supply of labour**. The supply of labour now exceeds the demand for labour and we have disequilibrium unemployment equal to Q1-Q2.

We are assuming that a rise in real wages does not cause a rise in productivity or consumer expenditure. If productivity, and/or consumption, did increase then the demand for labour would shift to the right and the rise in unemployment would be far smaller.

Policies to reduce real wage unemployment

Most prescriptions for reducing real wage unemployment centre around the idea of making each labour market more **flexible**, so that pay conditions become more adaptable to changing demand and supply conditions. Real wages should rise when demand, output and employment are rising, but they may need to fall if an industry experiences a recession which puts jobs at threat. Flexible labour markets involve working practices such as part-time and temporary contracts and shift work, as well as an absence of union power.

The national minimum wage (NMW) could be seen as a source of real wage employment. Supporters of flexible labour markets would argue for the abolition of minimum wages.

Frictional unemployment

This type of unemployment reflects **job turnover** in the labour market. Even when there are vacancies it takes people time to **search** and find a new job. During this period of time workers will remain frictionally unemployed.

Policies for frictional unemployment

- **Reduce Job Seeker's Allowance** (formerly unemployment benefit) – The job seeker has to show that he/she is **actively seeking work** and if they are unable to prove this at fortnightly interviews they lose their benefit. This measure was introduced to reduce the level of frictional unemployment. However, if the government reduced the level of the benefit, or limited the duration of a claim, search times between jobs could be reduced even further. This is because workers would have to take a job more quickly before their financial situations deteriorated. Some economists argue that if the unemployed were financially worse off they would not be able to search for work effectively. For example, they may not be able to afford to travel to interviews or telephone potential employers.

- **Direct tax cuts** – the government could reduce direct taxes for the low paid to increase the post tax wage and, therefore, encourage them to find work more quickly. Most analysts believe that tax cuts on their own are insufficient to reduce frictional unemployment. The benefit system needs to be reformed to eliminate the **unemployment trap** – this is a situation where someone is financially better off not working.

- **Improve job information** – facilities provided by job centres, private agencies, newspapers and the Internet. The development of the Job Centre Plus programme, which provides intensive support and advice for job seekers, is one way to help workers obtain employment more quickly.

Structural unemployment

Structural unemployment occurs when there is a mismatch between the characteristics of the unemployed and the characteristics needed in order to fill the vacancies in an economy.

Structural unemployment is caused by immobility of labour:

- **Occupational immobility** is associated with a lack of transferable skills, preventing workers from moving from one job to another.

- **Geographical immobility** prevents workers moving from one area to another in order to fill vacancies.

Structural unemployment is often centred on certain **regions** due to the long term decline of traditional manufacturing industries, such as coal, steel, textiles and shipbuilding. Employment in these sectors contracts due to intense overseas competition and the development of new technology.

Policies for the structural problem

There are a number of different approaches that can be adopted to help alleviate structural unemployment. These are sometimes known as **active labour market policies**.

- **Regional policy** – gives grants and tax breaks to encourage firms to locate in areas of high structural unemployment. This, however, does not solve the problem of **occupational immobility**. Regional policy often demands extra retraining schemes in order to give workers the relevant skills to allow them to take up new jobs.

Geographical immobility prevents workers moving from one area to another.

● **Investment in worker training** – The '**New Deal' programme**, launched in 1998, aims to provide a gateway back into employment for long term unemployed workers. The scheme has been modified over the years and now offers opportunities to job seekers of all ages. The scheme starts with an interview to identify any gaps in a worker's skills, training or knowledge. An individual programme is then developed for each participant. The options available within the programme include:

  ● subsidised employment

  ● work experience with employers

  ● training and help with basic skills

  ● a place on an environmental taskforce

  The aim of the scheme is to give workers the training and skills needed to take up jobs in their local areas. It is also hoped that real work experience will improve their **employability**.

● **Improving geographical mobility** – The government could provide grants or low cost housing to encourage workers to move from areas of high unemployment to regions where there are jobs. The problem with this policy is that people are inherently immobile because they are often bound by family and social ties.

● **The market solution** – one approach is simply to leave the problem of structural unemployment to the market. High unemployment will **drive down wages** and **new firms will be attracted into a region** to take advantage of the low costs of production. In this way the problem will eventually solve itself, but the **social deprivation created** in the short term may be considerable. Some commentators argue that intervention to solve structural unemployment slows the natural reallocation of resources to high growth areas and only makes the problem worse.

Causes of unemployment: summary	Demand or supply side?	Type	Cause
	Demand	Demand deficient	A lack of derived demand for labour, creating an output gap. Typically occurring during recession.
	Supply	Real wage	A real wage above the equilibrium in the labour market, generating an excess supply of labour.
	Supply	Frictional	Search periods between jobs, possibly reflecting a lack of information about vacancies or generous unemployment benefits.
	Supply	Structural	Mismatch caused by occupational and geographical immobility of labour.

The costs of unemployment

The costs of high levels of unemployment include:

● **Lost output** – unemployment causes a waste of scarce economic resources and reduces the growth potential of the economy. An economy with unemployment is producing inside its **production possibility frontier** (see Chapter 1). The hours that the unemployed do not work can never be recovered.

● **Impact on government expenditure, taxation and the budget deficit** – an increase in unemployment results in higher benefit payments and lower tax revenues. When individuals are unemployed, not only do they receive benefits but they pay no income tax. Because they are spending less, they contribute less to the government in indirect taxes. This rise in government spending, along with the fall in tax revenues, may result in a budget deficit (see Chapter 24).

● **Unemployment wastes some of the resources used in training workers.** Furthermore, workers who are unemployed for long periods become **de-skilled** as their skills become increasingly dated in a rapidly changing job market. This reduces their chances of gaining employment in the future, which in turn increases the burden on the government and the taxpayer.

● **Rising unemployment is linked to social and economic deprivation** – there is some relationship with crime and with social dislocation (increased divorce, worsening health and lower life expectancy). Areas of high unemployment will see falls in real incomes and an increase in income inequality.

Chapter

21

Unit 2: Measuring the macroeconomy → How the macroeconomy works →
Macroeconomic performance → Macroeconomic policy tools

Inflation

Definition of inflation	Inflation is a sustained increase in the general price level over a period of time. Inflation can be measured via the retail price index (RPI) or consumer price index (CPI). Further details can be found in Chapter 14.
Demand pull inflation	**Causes of Inflation** Demand pull inflation occurs when **total demand for goods and services exceeds total supply**. This type of inflation happens when there has been **excessive growth in aggregate demand** or when **current growth exceeds trend growth**.

Figure 21.1

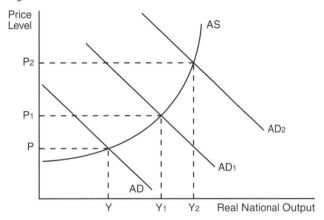

- At low levels of output when there is plenty of **spare productive capacity** (a substantial output gap) firms can easily expand output to meet increases in demand, resulting in a relatively elastic AS curve (see the shift from AD to AD_1, giving only moderate inflation of P to P_1).

- However, as the economy **approaches full capacity** and the output gap closes, labour and raw material shortages mean that it becomes more difficult for firms to expand production without pushing up their prices (see the shift from AD_1 to AD_2, giving more substantial inflation from P_1 to P_2).

- At the same time, many firms will choose to widen their **profit margins**. As a result, prices will rise sharply.

- It is likely that, as employment in the economy grows, demand for goods and services will become more inelastic. This will allow firms to pass on large price increases without any significant fall in demand.

Cost push inflation	This occurs when firms increase prices to maintain or protect profit margins after experiencing a rise in costs. The main causes are:

- Growth in **unit labour costs** – this occurs when average wages grow faster than productivity.

- Rising **input costs** – such as oil, raw materials and components.

- Increases in **indirect taxes** – VAT and excise duties are paid by producers and will, therefore, increase their costs.

- **Higher import prices** – a depreciation in the currency or a rise in world inflation rates will force up import prices.

Figure 21.2

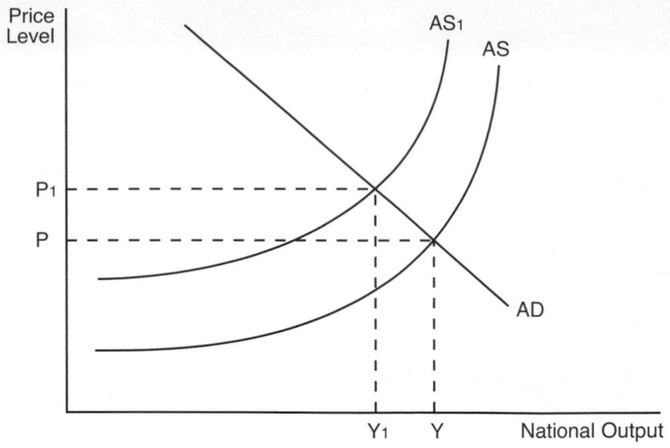

The effects of a rise in costs is illustrated in Figure 21.2.

● An increase in **input costs** will mean that firms can produce less at each and every price level and, as a result, the **aggregate supply curve will shift to the left** from AS to AS1.

● At the new equilibrium level of national output, the economy is producing a lower level of output (Y1) at a higher price level (P1). Higher cost push inflation therefore causes a contraction in real output as well as a higher price level.

● However, increases in the costs of firms do not always feed through to inflation. Firms may choose to absorb the increase in costs and accept reduced profit margins on each unit sold, especially when the consumer is very sensitive to price increases as may be the case during and immediately after a recession.

Stagflation

Figure 21.2 suggests that substantial cost increases **could** give rise to an unpleasant combination of economic circumstances. Rapidly rising oil prices, for example, could lead to a stagnating economy (**negative or sluggish growth with rising unemployment**) combined with high inflation. This is known as **stagflation**.

Policies to control inflation

A summary of policies that could be used to control inflation is given here. More detail on the main policy tools available for the government to influence the economy (fiscal, monetary and supply side policies) is given in Chapters 24, 25 and 26.

Policies to control inflation – summary

Demand side (short term) or supply side (long term)?	Policy type	Policy options
Demand side	Fiscal policy	Cut government spending or raise taxes in order to reduce consumption and restrict AD.
Demand side	Monetary policy	Raise interest rates in order to reduce consumption and investment, restricting AD.
		Engineer an exchange rate appreciation, reducing net exports (X-M) and restricting AD. This would also limit cost push by reducing the price of imported raw materials.
Supply side	Supply side policies	Market based reforms to increase productivity and create incentives to boost the trend growth rate of the economy.

Costs and effects of inflation

The costs and effects of inflation include:

1. Inflation distorts the operation of the price mechanism and can result in an **inefficient allocation of resources**. When inflation is volatile, consumers and firms are unlikely to have sufficient information on relative price levels to make informed choices about which products to purchase and supply.

2. **Effect on UK competitiveness** – if the UK has higher inflation than the rest of the world it will lose competitiveness in the international market. This assumes a given exchange rate. This rise in relative inflation leads to a fall in the world share of UK exports and a rise in import penetration. See Chapter 22 on the current account of the balance of payments. Ultimately, this will lead to a fall in the rate of economic growth and the level of employment.

3. **The problems of a wage-price spiral** – price rises can lead to higher wage demands as workers try to maintain their standard of living. This increases firms' costs and, in an effort to maintain their profit margins, they increase prices. The process could start all over again and inflation may get out of control. Higher inflation causes an upward shift in **inflationary expectations** that are then incorporated into wage bargaining. It can take some time for these expectations to be controlled.

4. **Reduction in the real value of savings** – especially if real interest rates (interest rates – inflation) are negative. This means the rate of interest does not fully compensate for the increase in the general price level. In contrast, **borrowers** see the **real value of their debt diminish**. Inflation, therefore, favours borrowers at the expense of savers.

5. **Consumers and businesses on fixed incomes will lose out.** Many pensioners are on fixed pensions so inflation reduces the real value of their income year on year. The state pension is normally increased each year in line with the RPI so that the real value of the pension is not reduced. However it is unlikely that pensioners have the same spending patterns as those used to create the weights from which the RPI figure is calculated. This may leave them worse off.

6. Inflation usually leads to **higher interest rates**, which will reduce economic growth and employment.

7. **Disruption of business planning** – high and volatile inflation creates uncertainty about the future. This makes planning and budgeting difficult as firms become unsure about what will happen to their costs. This could have a detrimental effect on investment in the economy. For example, if inflation is high and volatile, firms may demand a higher rate of return on investment projects before they will go ahead with the capital spending. These **hurdle rates** may cause projects to be cancelled or postponed until economic conditions improve. A low rate of capital investment clearly damages the productive potential of the economy and may reduce productivity growth.

8. Cost inflation usually leads to a slower growth of **profits** and this is likely to reduce the level of investment in the economy.

9. **Shoe leather costs** – when prices are unstable there will be an increase in search times to discover more about prices. Inflation increases the opportunity cost of holding money, so people make more visits to their banks and building societies (wearing out their shoe leather!).

10. **Menu costs** – are the extra costs to firms of changing price information.

Should there be a target rate of inflation?

There is a debate about whether having a target rate is helpful. On the one hand it may give policy credibility, reducing expectations of inflation, wage demands and therefore reducing inflation itself. On the other hand, governments may have to sacrifice economic growth to meet the target.

Chapter
22

Unit 2: Measuring the macroeconomy → How the macroeconomy works →
Macroeconomic performance → Macroeconomic policy tools

The current account of the balance of payments

The current account of the balance of payments

The current account primarily measures net trade in goods and services. For further details, see Chapter 14.

The current account and the economic cycle

The current account tends to **deteriorate** during the recovery phase of the business cycle and deteriorate to an even greater extent if this **recovery** becomes a **boom**. This is because growing income generates growing demand for goods and services. Inevitably this means growing demand for imports, both from consumers and firms. This is sometimes known as 'sucking in' imports.

The extent to which imports rise when incomes grow is measured by the **income elasticity of demand for imports**. This examines the responsiveness of the demand for imports to a change in the income of consumers. The income elasticity of demand for imports tends to rise when the economy is nearing full capacity, as it is increasingly difficult for demand to be met from domestic production.

While the current account deteriorates when income grows, it is likely to improve if incomes fall, resulting in lower demand for imports. Current account deficits can therefore be **cyclical**. A deficit that persists regardless of the stage of the economic cycle is known as a **structural deficit**.

Are current account deficits always a bad thing?

A common misconception is that current account deficits are always bad for the economy. This is not necessarily true. In the short term, if a country is importing a high volume of goods and services then this can boost **living standards**. It allows consumers to buy a higher level of **consumer durables** and other items. A cyclical current account deficit is generally not a concern.

However, in the long term a current account deficit may be a symptom of a weakening domestic economy and a **lack of international competitiveness**. It could be a sign of low levels of productivity and high domestic production costs, for example. If imports continue to rise, this will threaten domestic employment and incomes and **living standards may fall**.

For this reason, governments prefer to avoid substantial and persistent current account deficits (structural deficits).

Causes of a current account deficit

Some of the more common causes of a current account deficit are:

● **Growing income** – In recoveries and especially booms, when consumption and investment expenditure tend to rise, it is inevitable that some of this increased spending will leave the country as consumers and firms purchase imports. Other things being equal, this will cause the **current account balance to deteriorate**. The higher the income elasticity of demand for imports, the greater the increase in imports will be.

● **Lack of productive capacity of domestic firms** – If home producers have insufficient capacity to meet rising demand from consumers then imports of goods and services will come into the country to satisfy this excess demand. As a result, the current account will worsen.

● **Poor price and non price competitiveness** – Competitiveness can be measured by cost levels and domestic prices relative to international competitors, but non price factors are also important. These include quality, design, reliability and after-sales service. Inflation is a key determinant of international competitiveness. If the UK has higher inflation than the rest of the world has, it will lose competitiveness in international markets. Assuming that the quality of goods and services and the exchange rate remain unchanged, the rise in relative inflation will reduce UK exports and increase import penetration, and result in a deterioration of the current account.

- **Increased competition from other nations** – The advantages that countries have in producing certain goods and services can change over time, as technology alters and other countries exploit their economic resources and develop competing industries. The UK manufacturing sector, for example, has suffered over the last 25 years from the emergence of low cost production in newly industrialised countries.

- **An over-valued exchange rate** – Some economists believe that current account deficits stem from the exchange rate being at too high a level. A high exchange rate causes export prices to be higher in foreign markets whilst imports become relatively cheaper. Other things being equal, this will cause imports to rise, exports to fall and the current account balance to worsen.

- **Falling surplus in an important mineral resource** – Some countries rely heavily on the export of specific primary commodities whose prices on international markets might be highly volatile. A fall in price when demand from purchasers is inelastic can cause a sharp fall in total export revenues and a sudden deterioration in a country's current account.

Policies to reduce a current account deficit: expenditure reducing policies

Expenditure reducing policies aim to **reduce the spending of consumers and firms** so that the demand for imports falls. The following policies could be introduced:

- **Higher income taxes** will reduce real disposable incomes and should lead to a fall in expenditure on imports.

- **Higher interest rates** will discourage borrowing, increase saving and reduce consumers' real 'effective' disposable incomes. This should lead to a fall in consumer spending and a reduction in the level of imports.

The problem will these policies is that they only provide a **short term solution** and do not tackle the underlying causes of persistent account deficits (such as a lack of competitiveness). They also reduce aggregate demand and this will result in **lower economic growth and higher unemployment**.

Policies to reduce a current account deficit: expenditure switching policies

Expenditure switching policies attempt to encourage consumers to **switch** their demand away from imports and towards the output of domestic firms. This occurs if the price of imports can be raised, or if the price of UK products can be lowered. This change in relative prices should then cause a change in spending patterns in favour of output produced within the domestic economy. Expenditure switching policies include:

- A **devaluation** or **depreciation** of the exchange rate will reduce the price of exports and increase the price of imports. This policy will be most effective if the price elasticities of demand are high for both exports and imports, maximising the response of consumers and firms to the change in relative prices. This is more likely to be the case in the long run than in the short run, as it is more likely that spending patterns will adapt after a greater period of time has elapsed.

- The introduction of **tariffs** (a tax on imports) or other import controls will reduce imports (see Chapter 23). They will however raise prices for domestic consumers and may not be compatible with membership of organisations such as the EU and the World Trade Organisation.

- **Supply side policies** to improve **competitiveness**. The aim is to reduce unit costs of domestic firms, for example by encouraging greater investment and improved labour productivity. Measures to encourage innovation would also help improve competitiveness. Such policies take time to be effective, but address the underlying causes of persistent deficits. Economists would tend to look favourably at this way of switching expenditure towards domestically produced output.

Exchange rates

The process of international trade requires firms and consumers to use different currencies. The **exchange rate** can be defined simply as the price of one currency in terms of another.

Exchange rates are determined by the demand and supply of currencies on the foreign exchange markets. The demand and supply of currencies are determined by the following factors:

Demand for a currency	Supply of a currency
• exports of goods	• imports of goods
• exports of services	• imports of services
• inflows of direct investment	• outflows of direct investment
• inflows of portfolio investment and speculative demand for the currency	• outflows of portfolio investment and speculative selling of the currency
• official buying of the currency by the Central Bank	• official selling of the currency by the Central Bank

In Figure 23.1, the equilibrium exchange rate for the pound and the US dollar is at price P, where supply and demand for Sterling are equal.

If there is an **increase in demand** for the pound, due to a surge in exports to the USA, there will be **upward pressure** on the value of the exchange rate. In Figure 23.2, the demand for Sterling will shift to the right from D to D1 and the value of the pound will appreciate from P to P1. Conversely, if there is a fall in demand for Sterling, perhaps due to a fall in foreign direct investment from the USA, the demand for Sterling will shift from D to D2 and the currency will depreciate from P to P2.

An **increased supply of pounds**, due to a rise in imports from the USA, will apply **downward pressure** on the value of the currency. In Figure 23.3, the supply of Sterling will shift to the right from S to S1 and the value of the pound will depreciate from P to P1. Conversely, if there is a fall in supply for Sterling, perhaps due to a fall in speculative selling of the currency, the supply of Sterling will shift from S to S2 and the currency will appreciate from P to P2.

Figure 23.1

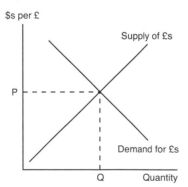

Figure 23.2

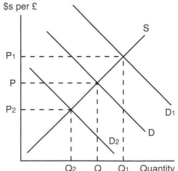

Figure 23.3

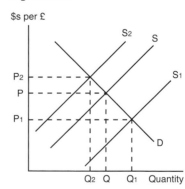

Chapter

24

Unit 2: Measuring the macroeconomy → How the macroeconomy works →
Macroeconomic performance → International trade → **Macroeconomic policy tools**

Fiscal policy

**Macro-
economic
policy**

**This box is repeated at the start of every chapter in the 'Macroeconomic policy tools'
section. You are recommended to read it each time.**

Macroeconomic policy tools are the instruments at the disposal of the government to help it achieve
its main economic objectives: strong, sustainable economic growth, low unemployment, low and
stable inflation, a satisfactory position on the current account of the balance of payments.

The main **demand side** policies are **fiscal policy and monetary policy**. The primary role for demand
side policies is to stabilise the economy in the short term, smoothing out the business cycle.

The successful application of demand side policies:

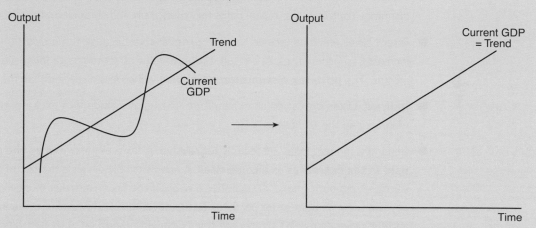

The role of **supply side policy** is to promote the long term health of the economy, boosting the trend
growth rate.

The successful application of supply side policies:

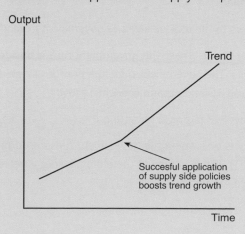

Fiscal policy	Fiscal policy involves the use of **government expenditure** and **taxation** to influence the level and composition of aggregate demand. A rise in government expenditure, or a fall in taxation, should increase aggregate demand and boost employment.
Useful definitions	● **General government expenditure** – consists of the combined **capital** and **current spending** of central and local government including debt interest. **Note the spending is split** into current spending on goods and services and capital expenditure on investment. The wages of teachers are an example of current spending, while the building of a school would constitute capital expenditure.

● **Transfer payments** are money transfers from the government to benefit recipients for which no output is produced. Examples include pensions, income support and job seeker's allowance.

● A tax is any **compulsory transfer** from a private individual, institution or group to central or local government.

● **Direct taxes** are taxes levied on income, wealth and profit. Examples include income tax, national insurance contributions, capital gains tax, council tax and corporation tax.

● Direct taxes, such as income tax, are **progressive** because the proportion of income paid in tax increases as income rises. As a result, progressive taxes act to reduce inequalities in the distribution of income. The **post-tax distribution of income** will be less dispersed than the **pre-tax distribution**.

● **Indirect taxes** are levied on expenditure. Examples include VAT, excise duties on fuel and alcohol, road tax and the TV licence.

● Generally, indirect taxes are seen as **regressive**. A tax is regressive when **the proportion of income paid in tax decreases as income rises**. A good example of this is the tax on cigarettes. Consider two smokers who both smoke 20 cigarettes a week. If the tax on a packet of cigarettes is £3 they will both pay the same amount of tax per week to the government. However, if one smoker earns £100 a week and the other earns £1000, they will pay a different proportion of their income in tax. The low-income smoker will pay 3% of their income (3/100 x 100), while the high-income smoker will pay 0.3% (3/1000 x 100). It is clear that the high-income smoker pays a lower proportion of their income in tax than the low-income smoker. A regressive tax therefore **widens the distribution of income**, which is seen by many as being undesirable.

● The **government's budget** refers to the relative levels of government expenditure and taxation.

● An **expansionary fiscal policy** is one where the government runs a **budget deficit**: government spending (G) exceeds taxation (T). The government therefore provides a net injection into the circular flow of income, serving to increase AD and expand economic activity.

● A **loosening of fiscal policy** involves raising G or cutting T.

● A **contractionary fiscal policy** is one where the government runs a **budget surplus**: taxation (T) exceeds government spending (G). The government therefore provides a net leakage from the circular flow of income, serving to reduce AD and economic activity.

● A **tightening of fiscal policy** involves cutting G or raising T.

Uses of fiscal policy: (1) influencing the level of demand and economic activity	One of the key uses of fiscal policy is to influence the level of aggregate demand. A **loosening of fiscal policy** such as an increase in government expenditure can be used to **stimulate current economic growth** and **generate employment**. This helps close large output gaps. A **tightening of policy** may be required to **control demand pull inflation** and **prevent the 'sucking in' of imports** due to high levels of aggregate demand.

In Figure 24.1, there is initially a sizeable output gap, representing spare capacity. An increase in government spending or a cut in taxation (thereby raising disposable income and consumption) is used to stimulate aggregate demand (AD → AD$_1$). **National output rises** (Y → Y$_1$) and this will generate an increased derived demand for labour **reducing demand deficient unemployment**. It is important to remember that the final change in national output will be greater than the initial stimulus to aggregate demand because of the operation of the multiplier process.

Figure 24.1

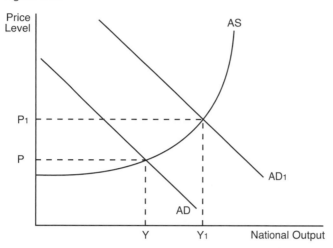

There are, however, potential difficulties with using fiscal policy to stimulate aggregate demand:

● **There is a danger of over stimulating the economy**, leading to inflationary pressure and a deterioration of the current account of the balance of payments. This danger increases as the economy nears full capacity.

An expansionary fiscal policy is where government spending exceeds taxation.

- **Governments need knowledge of the size of the output gap and the size of the multiplier** in order to judge how much to increase government expenditure. At best, the output gap and the size of the multiplier can only be estimated.

- **There are time lags involved in fiscal policy changes.** Major changes in fiscal policy are usually only made once a year, following the presentation of the government's budget. The full effects of any fiscal stimulus to AD will only be felt when the multiplier process has run its full course and this could take as long as two years.

- **'Crowding out' may occur.** This is when new government sector activity simply displaces private sector activity. If the government has to borrow to finance expenditure, this may force interest rates up, reducing private sector investment. This reduces the effectiveness of fiscal policy and may be thought undesirable because the government tends to use resources less efficiently than the private sector due to a lack of a profit motive.

Uses of fiscal policy: (2) influencing the composition of demand and economic activity

The pattern of spending in a market economy may generate an inefficient allocation of resources (market failure). The government may use fiscal policy to try to **correct some market failures** by encouraging spending on some products and discouraging spending on others:

- **Public goods** such as street lighting and the national defence system would not be provided by the private sector due to the free-rider problem stemming from the non-rivalrous and non-excludable nature of the good. This creates a clear need for government expenditure to fund state provision of the goods concerned.

- **Merit goods** would be provided by the private sector, but not in sufficient quantities. Goods that are associated with positive externalities are often subsidised or provided by the state.

- In contrast, the government may use indirect taxes to discourage the consumption of **demerit goods**, such as alcohol and tobacco, and to deter **polluting activities** that contribute to environmental damage.

The government may also wish to use fiscal policy to shift the balance of aggregate demand away from consumption and towards investment in order to boost the long term performance of the economy. It may offer tax breaks on profits that firms retain to use for investment purposes, for example.

Uses of fiscal policy (3): the redistribution of income and wealth

Many people consider that the market economy fails to produce equitable outcomes and that a highly unequal distribution of income and wealth is unfair and constitutes a **market failure**.

This justifies government intervention to make the distribution of income and wealth more equal. With regard to income, for example, the UK operates a **progressive taxation system**. This takes a higher proportion of the incomes of high income earners than it does from lower earners. Some of the benefits available through the social security system are only available to those whose incomes are low enough to qualify (**means tested benefits**). Thus fiscal policy is used to redistribute income.

Uses of fiscal policy (4): paying for government

Even in a pure market economy, there are some essential roles for the government such as protecting property rights, preserving the rule of law, issuing currency and so on. Taxation must be levied to pay for the bodies necessary to carry out these roles, such as the police and the courts. There are also a number of regulatory bodies (such as utility regulators like OFGEM) that require financing.

Chapter

25

Unit 2: Measuring the macroeconomy → How the macroeconomy works →
Macroeconomic performance → International trade → **Macroeconomic policy tools**

Monetary policy

**Macro-
economic
policy**

This box is repeated at the start of every chapter in the 'Macroeconomic policy tools' section. You are recommended to read it each time.

Macroeconomic policy tools are the instruments at the disposal of the government to help it achieve its main economic objectives: strong, sustainable economic growth, low unemployment, low and stable inflation, a satisfactory position on the current account of the balance of payments.

The main **demand side** policies are **fiscal policy and monetary policy**. The primary role for demand side policies is to stabilise the economy in the short term, smoothing out the business cycle.

The successful application of demand side policies:

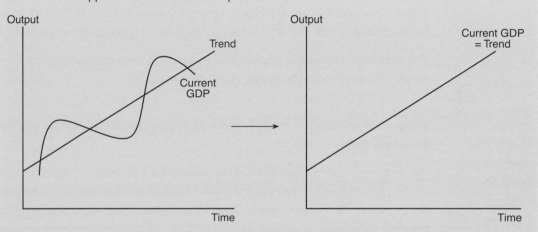

The role of **supply side policy** is to promote the long term health of the economy, boosting the trend growth rate.

The successful application of supply side policies:

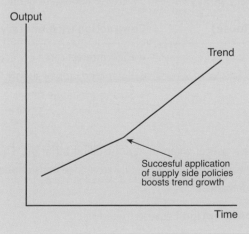

Monetary policy

Monetary policy can be used to influence aggregate demand and inflation. It covers:

- **Interest rates**
- **The money supply**
- **The exchange rate**

In general, interest rates measure the **rate of return on savings** and the **cost of borrowed money**. There is clearly more than one interest rate in the economy. Secured loans (such as mortgages – the house can be repossessed if the borrower fails to meet repayments) carry a lower rate of interest than unsecured personal loans, which carry a greater risk to the lender. Credit cards carry a high rate of interest. This is the price the borrower pays for 'borrowing on demand'. Financial intermediaries such as banks and building societies charge higher rates to borrowers than they do to savers. However, the government (or the central bank on its behalf – the Bank of England in the UK) sets the official base rate for the economy and this influences other interest rates.

There is no single definition of the money supply but, as well as notes and coins in circulation, it includes deposits that are available to be spent such as those in the current account of bank customers. Banks are able to add to the money supply by creating deposits when they make loans to customers.

The exchange rate is the price of one currency in terms of another, determined by the demand and supply of currencies on the foreign exchange markets.

Contractionary and expansionary monetary policies

When monetary policy is used to restrict aggregate demand it is known as a **contractionary or tight monetary policy**.

The three elements of a tight monetary policy are a high interest rate, a restricted money supply and a strong exchange rate. In practice these three components are linked. A high interest rate tends to restrict the growth of the money supply because there is a lower demand for loans and this restricts the ability of banks to create new deposits. A high interest rate also strengthens the exchange rate by encouraging a higher demand for the currency from those living overseas who wish to earn a high interest rate on their money.

An **expansionary** or **loose monetary policy** serves to increase aggregate demand.

Expansionary monetary policy (loose)	Contractionary monetary policy (tight)
• Low interest rate	• High interest rate
• Money supply allowed to grow	• Restricted money supply
• Weak exchange rate	• Strong exchange rate

Monetary policy and inflation

A tightening of monetary policy is a useful weapon in controlling inflation. The chosen policy tool is commonly raising the official base rate. The aim is primarily to reduce consumption and investment, the two key components of aggregate demand.

Higher interest rates will **reduce consumption** because there will be:

- **a rise in saving**. This is because the opportunity cost of spending has increased.
- **a fall in the demand for consumer durables purchased on credit**. This is because loan repayments will increase.
- **a fall in 'discretionary incomes'**. Rising mortgage payments will reduce the ability of homeowners to spend.

An expansionary monetary policy serves to increase aggregate demand.

Investment may also fall, as the costs of borrowing funds will increase. Some investment projects will become unprofitable and will not be undertaken.

Aggregate demand shifts to the left, controlling inflation. However, there are some problems to note:

● Tighter monetary policy restricts economic growth.

● Monetary policy is less effective in controlling cost push inflation than in controlling demand pull inflation.

● Although monetary policy begins to act quickly as higher mortgage repayments immediately begin to squeeze discretionary incomes, there are still time lags involved, such as the time needed for the multiplier effect to run its course. Changes to policy may take around 18 months to have their full effect and by then economic circumstances may have changed.

Monetary policy and economic growth

A loosening of monetary policy could be used to promote current economic growth. Lower interest rates mean cheaper credit, lower mortgage repayments and less attractive returns on saving. Consumption is likely to be boosted. Investment is likely to rise too as the cost of borrowed funds falls.

Aggregate demand shifts to the right, raising the current rate of growth. Drawbacks include the danger of demand pull inflation and the 'sucking in' of imports as income grows.

Should the target of monetary policy be inflation or growth?

The benefit of targeting a particular rate of inflation is that it may help create **credibility**. Economic agents may come to expect inflation to be low and stable. This encourages low wage settlements, **preventing wage-price spirals**. Low and stable inflation also gives firms the confidence to invest.

The drawback of targeting inflation is that interest rates may be higher than they would otherwise be, thus restricting current growth. In times of economic downturn, the only policy tool then available to the government to support growth is fiscal policy. If the government's financial position does not allow it to raise spending then slow or negative economic growth may result. This creates a possible case for using monetary policy to support current economic growth rather than exclusively targeting a particular inflation rate.

Chapter 26

Unit 2: Measuring the macroeconomy → How the macroeconomy works →
Macroeconomic performance → International trade → **Macroeconomic policy tools**

Supply side policy

Macro-economic policy

This box is repeated at the start of every chapter in the 'Macroeconomic policy tools' section. You are recommended to read it each time.

Macroeconomic policy tools are the instruments at the disposal of the government to help it achieve its main economic objectives: strong, sustainable economic growth, low unemployment, low and stable inflation, a satisfactory position on the current account of the balance of payments.

The main **demand side** policies are **fiscal policy and monetary policy**. The primary role for demand side policies is to stabilise the economy in the short term, smoothing out the business cycle.

The successful application of demand side policies:

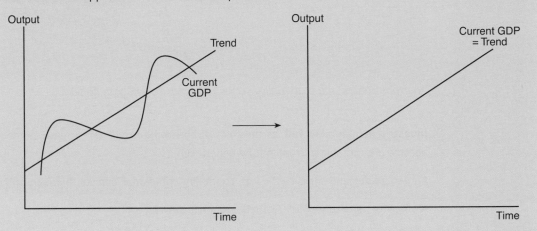

The role of **supply side policy** is to promote the long term health of the economy, boosting the trend growth rate.

The successful application of supply side policies:

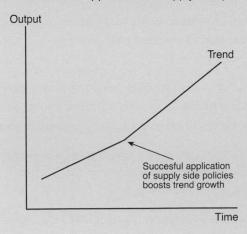

Supply side policies

Supply side policies are policies that aim to:

● **increase productivity**

● **improve incentives** and

● **improve the efficiency of resource allocation** in order to **boost the trend growth rate** (potential growth) of the economy and shift the aggregate supply curve to the right.

A distinctive feature of supply side policies is that they usually involve reducing the role of the government in the economy. Supply side policies are market orientated policies that reflect a belief that the private sector of the economy uses resources more efficiently than the public (government) sector.

It is important to remember that the trend (potential) growth rate of the economy reflects the rate at which the economy's capacity grows and that capacity is a function of the quantity and quality of the four factors of production: land, labour, capital and enterprise.

Figure 26.1 shows the effects of the successful application of supply side policies.

Figure 26.1

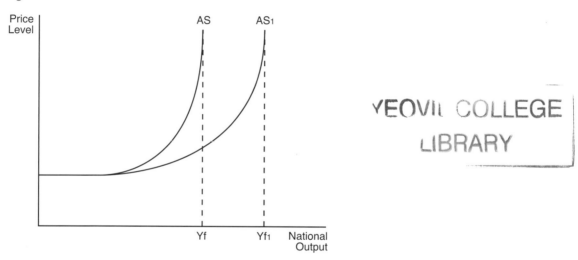

(1) Labour market policies

Supply side policies in the labour market aim to improve the skills of the labour force (**human capital**), promote **labour mobility**, **remove barriers** that prevent wages reaching equilibrium levels and encourage **flexible working practices** (part-time work, shift work, temporary contracts) that help control costs of production. Specific examples include:

● Income tax cuts to improve incentives to work.

● Cuts in benefit payments to make voluntary unemployment less affordable.

● Tax relief on income earned from renting out accommodation. The rented housing sector promotes labour mobility.

● Removal of the national minimum wage so that the labour market can reach equilibrium.

● Measures to reduce the power of trade unions.

● Reduced government regulation of labour markets to lower the non-wage costs of taking on workers.

● Financial help for firms that invest in the training of workers.

● Changes to the education system to broaden access to further and higher education and to promote vocational training.

(2) Product market policies	Product market policies aim to offer encouragement to private sector firms and to promote competition. Examples include: ● Privatisation, such as the sale of state owned firms to private shareholders. ● Deregulation of markets to open them up to new competition. This occurred in the UK gas and electricity markets, which were at one time statutory monopolies with a single supplier. ● Tax relief on profits retained by firms for investment purposes.
(3) Policies in financial markets	It is important that firms have access to finance in order to invest and innovate. Supply side policies in this area focus on making finance more readily available. One example in the UK was the creation of the Alternative Investment Market (AIM) to allow firms not yet ready to be listed on the Stock Exchange to raise share capital.
(4) Policies to encourage enterprise	Policies to encourage enterprise include: ● Low corporation tax, to increase the profit incentive and stimulate investment. ● Reduced regulation of business. The rules imposed on business by government are sometimes known as 'red tape' and the aim of supply side policies would be to reduce these bureaucratic requirements. Even the length of time to go through the administrative processes of starting up a company can vary widely from country to country. ● Patents to allow those who innovate to exploit the commercial potential of their ideas free from competition for an initial period of time.
Potential benefits of supply side policies	Supply side policies are often thought vital to the long term health of the economy. While **demand side** policies can be used to **stabilise** the economy in the short run, increasing **long run prosperity** depends primarily on the **trend growth rate**. By boosting the **trend growth rate**, supply side policies have the potential to improve simultaneously all the four main macroeconomic objectives. The increased capacity of the economy allows a higher GDP to be generated. This will boost **economic growth**. **Unemployment will fall**, as higher output in the economy will generate an increased demand for labour. Higher capacity and improved efficiency will lower costs and dampen **cost push inflationary pressure**. This helps **improve price competitiveness**, while some of the new capacity can be used to serve the export market. This **improves the current account** of the balance of payments.
Potential costs of supply side policies	Supply side policies are not a solution to all economic ills. They **do not act quickly**; demand side policies are more appropriate for stabilising the economy when a rapid response is needed. Furthermore, in practice **increases in an economy's trend growth rate are very difficult** to bring about and after years of supply side measures, UK labour productivity still lags behind other leading nations, such as the USA and Germany. A further problem with supply side policies is that, while they may be **efficient**, it is a matter of opinion as to whether they are **equitable**. For example, flexible working practices benefit some people (such as parents with childcare commitments to juggle) but leave others exposed to insecurity, not knowing how long their employment will last and how many hours they will be asked to work in a week. Supply side measures, such as reductions in trade union power and abolishing minimum wages, also leave workers vulnerable. It is possible that there is an **equity-efficiency trade-off** in the labour market.